Praise for *Bridge to the Afterlife*

"I have to admit I was a bit skeptical when I first discovered Troy was a medium. But then I saw him in action and read his book, and now I believe there is more out there than meets the eye. *Bridge to the Afterlife* is a compelling and believable story. Troy shares his own skepticism and, finally, his acceptance of a power he cannot fully explain."
—*Dale Bosch, Bosch Media, executive producer for Discovery Health Channel's* House of Babies *and The History Channel's* MonsterQuest

"Troy's messages of hope and love from the other side of the veil are life transforming. I highly recommend reading his book and sharing it with loved ones—realizing that it is love that never dies."
—*Barbara Moore, owner of*
The Dragonfly Ranch Healing Arts Center, Hawaii

"Troy Parkinson's journey to mediumship is a fascinating read. His many encounters with spirit guides led him to change careers and accept mediumship as his calling. Since then, he has helped many of the bereaved find closure with loved ones that have crossed over."
—*Gary and Insiah Beckman, president and vice president of Leap Publications, Inc., producers of Edge Life Expos and Events*

"Troy Parkinson beautifully explains the life of the spirit communicator."
—*Rita S. Berkowitz, the Spirit Artist and co-author of*
The Complete Idiot's Guide to Communicating with Spirits

"This book will help the developing medium understand some of the trials and tribulations involved in the process of unfoldment, as well as the joy one achieves when stepping upon the threshold of life and allowing spirit that is out of physical form to communicate with spirit in body."
—*Rev. Simeon Stefanidakis, Pastor, Albertson Memorial Church of*
Spiritualism, Old Greenwich, CT, and author of
How to Develop Mediumship *and* Journey of the Soul

Bridge to the
Afterlife

About the Author

Troy Parkinson began studying the afterlife in the late 1990s at the First Spiritual Temple in Boston. He returned to Fargo, North Dakota, in 2000, where he continues his work as a medium. Troy has traveled throughout the United States, spoken at various holistic expos, and been featured by numerous publications and radio programs.

As a filmmaker, Troy has worked as a writer/producer/director for cable networks such as Discovery Health Channel and The History Channel. His ultimate goal as a filmmaker is to create spiritually driven projects. He was one of the first participants in producer Stephen Simon's Spiritual Cinema telecourses, and has been the point person for the state of North Dakota in hosting special screenings of spiritually themed films.

Troy's mission in this life is to bring focus to the spirit, mind, and body. You can visit him online at www.troyparkinson.com.

To Write to the Author

If you wish to contact the author or would like more information about this book, please write to the author in care of Llewellyn Worldwide and we will forward your request. Both the author and publisher appreciate hearing from you and learning of your enjoyment of this book and how it has helped you. Llewellyn Worldwide cannot guarantee that every letter written to the author can be answered, but all will be forwarded. Please write to:

Troy Parkinson
% Llewellyn Worldwide
2143 Wooddale Drive, Dept. 978-0-7387-1435-6
Woodbury, Minnesota 55125-2989, U.S.A.
Please enclose a self-addressed stamped envelope for reply,
or $1.00 to cover costs. If outside U.S.A., enclose
international postal reply coupon.

Many of Llewellyn's authors have websites with additional information and resources. For more information, please visit our website at http://www.llewellyn.com

TROY PARKINSON

Bridge to the
Afterlife

A Medium's Message of Hope & Healing

Llewellyn Publications
Woodbury, Minnesota

First Edition
First Printing, 2009

Book design by Steffani Sawyer
Cover design by Kevin R. Brown
Cover photo © 2009 by iStockphoto.com/Narvikk
Llewellyn is a registered trademark of Llewellyn Worldwide, Ltd.

Library of Congress Cataloging-in-Publication Data

Parkinson, Troy, 1977–
  Bridge to the afterlife : a medium's message of hope & healing / Troy Parkinson.—1st ed.
      p. cm.
  Includes bibliographical references.
  ISBN 978-0-7387-1435-6
  1. Parkinson, Troy, 1977– 2. Mediums—United States—Biography.
3. Spiritualism. I. Title.
  BF1283.P37A3 2009
  133.9'1092—dc22
  [B]
                                        2009001606

Llewellyn Publications
A Division of Llewellyn Worldwide, Ltd.
2143 Wooddale Drive, Dept. 978-0-7387-1435-6
Woodbury, Minnesota 55125-2989, U.S.A.
www.llewellyn.com

Printed in the United States of America

To Chanda and Jacob,
Thanks for choosing me again.
You bring such love and joy to my life.

Contents

Preface

Quite honestly, I didn't know what to expect. I suppose nobody truly knows what it will be like the first time they choose to skydive. Of course, what person in their right mind would consciously choose to voluntarily jump from an airplane at fourteen thousand feet? It was a question I was beginning to ask myself as I signed a release form stating, IF YOU DIE, WE ARE NOT RESPONSIBLE. Here I was, a husband and a father of a three-and-a-half year old, and I was signing a document stating that if I died jumping from an airplane, my family could not do anything about it.

As I continued to receive my brief orientation on the do's and don'ts of a tandem skydive, I thought back to the jump I had made four weeks earlier. I had just left my full-time job as a film and television producer for a company I'd worked at for the last seven years. During my tenure at the company, I had been involved with a number of projects with companies like Microsoft, Bobcat, *Inside Edition*, and Subway. I also was instrumental in my company's cable television endeavors; I had produced a daytime series for Discovery Health Channel called *House of Babies* and field produced a few episodes of the History Channel series *MonsterQuest*. My life as a television producer was great, and the opportunities were endless. Yet I choose to leave it all, to go out on my own and embrace my other calling... being a medium.

Yes. I, like the kid in the movie, could "see dead people." This ability to connect with the other side had been developing for years, and so when the inspiration came to take my family on a six-week adventure down the Pacific Coast to share my work as a medium, I followed it. We started with a road trip from Portland to L.A., then added a stint in Hawaii and finally two weeks of traveling across Montana.

I'm choosing to follow my inspiration and live life full-out as a medium, I thought to myself. *What am I, crazy?* Clearly, I must be crazy. I was not only choosing to leave the security of a full-time job (with a 401k, health insurance, etc.), but I was also strapping myself into a harness that would be attached to the skydiver I was about to jump out of an airplane with. In my mind, I had always imagined that a tandem jump required hours of training. Instead, I'd watched a brief orientation video and met my tandem guide minutes before we walked on the plane. As we were taking off, he filled me in on all I needed to do.

As we ascended to our jump altitude, I couldn't help but be mesmerized by the beauty all around me. For the past four weeks I had been traveling down the Pacific Coast with my family, but this was by far one of the most incredible things I'd seen yet. I was flying over the north end of Oahu, in Hawaii, witnessing the magnificent colors of the ocean, the green lush mountains, and nothing but sandy beaches for miles. If there is such a thing as heaven on earth, then this moment was it.

However, that moment of bliss didn't last too long. The next thing I knew, the side door of the plane was thrust open and the roar of the wind filled the fuselage. Two by two, people were suddenly jumping out of the plane. *Oh, my god. This was happening. There was no turning back now.* As I found myself on deck, my tandem partner yelled, "Remember—if you can't breathe, it's because *you* are not breathing. Just breathe like normal and *don't hold your breath.*"

We inched our way to the edge of the door, and my cameraman jumped first. Being an eternal documentarian, I of course had sprung the extra cash to have my jump captured on film. I figured this was a once-in-a-lifetime experience, so I better have the pictures to remember it.

In the moments before the leap, as I peered out into that beautiful blue sky, I realized that this must be what it's like before a spirit comes to the earth to be born. It also must be what it is like for a spirit when they return to heaven. It is a moment of pure excitement and pure uncertainty. On one hand, you know this is going to be an experience like no other, but there is also an ounce of fear, and suddenly you're filled with all the "what ifs." *What if this doesn't go how I planned? What if the people I'm hoping to see aren't there? What if everything I've been told isn't true? What if…*"

"Three—two—one—jump!" We made the leap, and the free fall began. In those first ten to fifteen seconds, the only thing going through my mind was *Holy sh#! What the #$%★ did I just do?* My mind was racing, I couldn't breathe, my sinuses were all congested, and I had to clear my throat. I tried to spit, only to realize that when you're falling at 120 miles per hour, spit doesn't go away from your face—it ends up all over it. Thank God I was wearing goggles. As we continued to fall, I realized I wasn't breathing. I instantly remembered the words of my faithful guide: "If you can't breathe, you are not breathing." With that I took in a big deep breath and realized there was nothing I could *do* now. All I could do was *be*.

As I fell through the air, my life flashed before my eyes. Moments from my childhood, adolescence, and adulthood played out in front of me like a movie—the highs, the lows, the joys, the sorrow. But the moments that resonated the most were the ones of service. Moments when I was in service to others, moments when I shared messages of hope and healing, moments when I was a true bridge for spirit. This realization created a moment of pure bliss, complete awe, and the peaceful realization that if I was intended to die falling out of this plane, then I would die; but if I didn't, it would be the universe's way of letting me know I still had work to do here on Earth. I was to continue my soul's mission of connecting people to their loved ones in spirit.

Suddenly, my tandem guide pulled the cord and the parachute deployed. It was almost as though he had heard my thoughts and knew he had to get me to the ground safely. As we floated down in the paradise, the stillness was miraculous, and my connection to the abundant glory of creation all around me had never been so profound. When I made it to the ground, I kissed my wife, hugged my son, and knew life would never be the same.

Introduction

The following is a journey ... a journey that forever changed my life and continues to transform it daily. What you will find in these pages is an account of my adventure into the fascinating world of mediumship and spirit communication—from my initial experience as a child in North Dakota, to my two years with the First Spiritual Temple in Boston, and back again.

Of course, you have to understand that when this journey began, I never thought I'd be writing this book. As a kid growing up, I wanted to be a police officer, or a biologist, or even a professional baseball player. Ultimately, I found my passion for creative expression in film production and spent most of my junior high and high school years behind a video camera making the next big movie. The idea that I'd grow up to be a medium was something that had never entered my mind. It's not to say I wasn't interested in the idea of what happens to us when we die. I'd seen mediums on TV and read books on near death experiences … I guess I just always thought it was an ability the "gifted" had, not something I could or would ever possess. But here I am, and here you are.

I've written this book in three sections. Part One, *The Journey,* is an account of how I came to discover my connection to the other side. Part Two, *The Messages,* takes a look at some of the most powerful messages that have come forward through my experience. Part Three, *What's It All Mean?* is where I reflect on the impact mediumship has had on my life and some of the things I've learned along the journey. I also provide you with some practical exercises to help in your own development of mediumship.

As I was writing this book, I was able to reach back and read through old journals and review various video and audio recordings from past readings. The experience was very enlightening, and I found myself reconnecting to the faces and places that have had such an impact on my life. The individual experiences reported in this book are true, and, wherever possible, I transcribed spirit messages directly from audio recordings of the sessions. Some families and individuals allowed me to include their complete stories and names. However, in some cases, names and descriptive details have been adjusted to protect personal identities.

There is one thing I want to stress. I believe that mediumship is an ability we *all* have; it is not something given to the "spiritually elite." You also don't need a profound metaphysical experience or to have some dramatic accident to tap into your own connection with spirit. Making the link simply takes practice. It's like any other muscle in your body—with consistent exercise and dedication, anyone can strengthen their mediumistic or intuitive muscle and build that bridge to the afterlife.

What follows is my story...a story that can occur for any of you and, for some, maybe already has. Recognizing and establishing your link to spirit is one of the most rewarding experiences you can have. I hope my story will also offer you new inspiration for your spiritual journey—that it may remind you of how close your loved ones in spirit truly are, and that their souls do live on.

Troy Parkinson
August 2008

PART ONE

The Journey

chapter

1

A Journey Begins

Some people believe we choose the area of the world we wish to grow up in, before we are born. For others, it's just a random experience; you end up where you are because that is where your parents lived. I like to think that the collective consciousness of a city is what ultimately draws you to a location. From the spot you were born, to the city you were raised in, to all the places you've ever lived, each location draws you in and provides opportunities and experiences that no other area could provide. Some people resist and run from their hometowns, while others never leave. I've done both.

On a soul level, I know that Fargo, North Dakota, was one city I was destined to be a resident of. Yes, I'm from Fargo. Yes … just like the movie. And yes, some people from this neck of the woods actually do talk like that, don't ya know. Being raised in Fargo was a wonderful experience; although, for most of my life when I said I was from Fargo, people would ask, "Where?" So in 1996, when the Coen brothers released the movie *Fargo*, I was actually grateful to have a film named after our city. It put us in the public eye and in the heart of pop culture. Not everyone from this area likes the movie, but just for the record, I love it! I even helped with the event planning for the *Fargo* DVD release party … but that's another story.

I was born in Minot, North Dakota, on December 5, 1977, at 3:19 AM. That makes me a Sagittarius sun sign with Libra rising. According to my parents, it was cold those early morning hours of December 5, and I was born within forty-five minutes of arriving at the hospital. I was the second child in our family; my brother, Shawn, was five years older than me. My father, Dennis, sold insurance, and my mother, Corine, was a stay-at-home mom. For the first two years of my life we lived in Minot, North Dakota, ultimately moving to Fargo in 1979. I don't remember much from those first years, of course, and my family doesn't recall any unique or strange abilities I had as a toddler. I did play baby Jesus in the 1977 church Christmas pageant, but I'm sure it's because I was the only newborn available.

As a medium, people often ask me if I was born with this ability and if I have always seen spirit. I'm always torn on how to answer this question, because as a kid I didn't see spirits the way I see them now; in fact, it wasn't until college that I fully discovered my abilities. But I can't deny a profoundly vivid experience I had as a young child.

A Midnight Visit

When I was five years old, my life was a constant whirlwind. I played with friends, started school, and didn't really think about ghosts unless they were chasing Shaggy and Scooby in the cartoons. Yet one evening, my thoughts about spirit changed forever.

It was the middle of the night, and for some reason I was compelled to wake up from my deep sleep. I remember slowly opening my eyes and feeling as though there was someone else in the room. I rolled over to see if my brother was next to me, but he was not. Confused, I rolled back to my original position and closed my eyes. Suddenly, I felt a presence again. This time I slowly sat up in my bed, and when I looked across the room I observed something I'll never forget.

There, sitting on my desk, was the young boy. It was as if time had stopped and I was moving through a slow-motion experience. I couldn't make out the boy's facial features; all I could see was a glowing silhouette of white light. He was sitting with his legs hanging over the side of the desk, and his arms were folded over each other like a genie. His little presence illuminated my room.

Although I didn't feel threatened by his presence, I was shocked. My heart was pounding with such speed I thought for sure it was going to leap out of my chest. In that moment I did the only thing I could think of—I shoved my head under my covers and stayed hidden for as long as I could. Somehow I believed my covers had the power of a stone wall or a force field, and if I stayed covered the little boy would go away. Finally, at some point, I fell back to sleep. But the experience lingered, and the next morning I told my mom about what I had seen.

She responded very positively. I appreciated that she chose not to belittle my experience by telling me it was a dream. Instead, she suggested that maybe what I saw was an angel coming down to protect me. Having been raised in a Christian household, I was used to the idea of angels and recalled hearing about them in Bible stories and Sunday school.

At the time, my mother's explanation comforted me, and as I reflect back on it now, I do know it was a spirit making a connection with me. My experience is similar to what many of my clients have experienced as children. People I've spoken with tend to recall seeing spirits when they were young, but as they grew up they blocked out the communication. In many respects, I believe this spirit was simply watching over me, protecting me while I slept. It was an event that has forever impacted me. I saw a being of light, a child spirit with the peace and wisdom of a sage. But why me? Why then? I would spend the next twenty-five years of my life trying to answer those questions.

• • •

Time passed, and I went through elementary school with no more encounters. As I continued to grow, my mind started to try to understand the concept of spirits and God. My friends and I would even try little tricks to test God. I remember one time when we were outside and the wind was blowing—so in our defiant way we told God, "If you're there, stop the wind!"

Nothing happened, and the wind still blew.

Again we asked, "God, if you're there, stop the wind."

We paused... again nothing happened.

Finally we demanded, "God, if you're there, STOP THE WIND!"

And just as we finished the sentence, the wind stopped.

Needless to say, in that moment we were amazed and somewhat spooked. I'm sure we continued the test throughout the rest of the afternoon, trying to see how many times the wind would stop. Now, whether it was coincidence, or God, or both, one could say that my conversations with spirit had begun. Just not in the way they do today.

My First Encounters with Death

I know for any parent, one of the hardest parts of raising a child is trying to explain what happens when you die. Being raised Methodist and Lutheran, I was taught that when you die you go to be with God and Jesus in heaven. This belief and faith in an afterlife created a sense of comfort around death, since we all believed we'd go on to a better place. As a result, my family always maintained a sense of humor about death and dying.

I recall that on one of my first visits to the cemetery, my family chose to keep things light rather than somber and melodramatic. I was four or five years old and we were visiting relatives on my mom's side of the family. When our family was together, we'd go honor our relatives with a visit to their gravesites. When we arrived at the cemetery, all the cousins crawled out of the car and, since I was the youngest, I did my best to catch up.

As I was running up to my cousins, my dad yelled out, "Troy, slow down or you'll walk on the bodies."

I stopped dead in my tracks and said, "What?"

My brother Shawn added, "Yeah, Troy, watch out or you'll walk on the people." He proceeded to point out all the headstones and the areas where the bodies were.

I wasn't scared by what they were saying, just more focused on not stepping on the graves. As a result, I was like a soldier trying to avoid mines in a minefield. There I was, tiptoeing around, trying to avoid stepping on anyone and jumping from here to there in an effort to get to our relative's headstone. I felt like I was in the 1980s video game *Frogger*—I was strategically moving from left to right and back again. Ultimately, my mother came to my rescue and told me not to worry about it, that I could walk normally. The family had a good laugh at my expense.

I also attended a few funerals of distant relatives when I was young. I remember seeing the body of a deceased relative and hearing my mother state that the body was just a shell and the spirit was now living in heaven. Seeing the embalmed body didn't scare me; in fact, I was curious and wanted to touch its hand. The waxy feeling of the skin made my relative appear more like a mannequin than a living person. However, since these loved ones were people I really didn't know or have a strong emotional connection to, the concept of what it meant to lose a loved one hadn't registered yet.

It wasn't until I realized that my own mother could and would die that the fear of death came into my awareness. This conceptual understanding of death occurred in the strangest of all places. I don't recall what brought it on, but I found myself crying at my brother's football game, for it was at that moment I realized that one day my mom would die and I would be without her. It was a profound and terrifying thought. How could it be possible that she could be right next to me one minute and then gone the next minute? The thought of never seeing my mother again brought on more tears.

My mother kept telling me she wasn't going to die. Maybe that's what any parent would say in the moment. Maybe that's what I'll say to my own son when he comes to understand the concept of death. As I continued to cry, other families around us began to wonder what was wrong.

But no amount of reassuring helped. I now understood death and was grief stricken and scared at the thought of a life without my mother or my father. Who would be there to support me? Who would be there to hug me? Who would be there to let me know everything was going to be okay? Maybe there was a heaven, but I didn't think it was fair that God would take my mother and father away. It was the thought of not being able to talk to them that hurt the most.

Thankfully, my mother didn't die. However, what did die that day was my innocence about death. The reality of what it would mean to lose someone close to me finally registered, and I didn't want to face the death of a loved one. Yet despite my desire to avoid the death experience, I had to face my fears a few years later when my grandparents passed away.

Grandpa and Grandma Parkinson

To understand my connection to my grandpa and grandma Parkinson, you have to know a little bit about the geography of North Dakota. My grandparents lived in the small town of Kenmare, which is located about forty-five minutes northwest of Minot (where I was born), but almost six hours from Fargo (in the eastern part of the state, where I grew up). Kenmare is nestled on the Des Lacs National Wildlife Refuge and contains great rolling hills—a dramatic contrast to the flat plains of Fargo. Grandpa and Grandma Parkinson also had a special place in my heart because I only saw them three or four times a year.

My grandpa was a farmer and my grandmother a farm wife. They were a hard-working couple who raised four children: my aunt, my twin uncles, and my father. My grandfather, Leonard, was a big man, the stoic type with a gruff voice and silver hair that he combed back. He came from a big family and was the oldest, which meant that when his own father died at age fifty-five, my grandfather had to become the man of the family at only fifteen. He worked as a farmer his entire life. As a result, he had mangled, arthritic-ridden hands that always looked a little scary to a kid. Clearly his hands were the things I remembered most because at one point in my childhood, I had a pair of oversized work gloves on my hands. The fingers wouldn't stay up and they looked crooked.

I lifted my hands up and said to my mom and dad, "Hey look, guys...it's Grandpa Parkinson's hands."

Both of my parents laughed, and it was pretty much agreed that my Grandpa had some very unique hands.

My grandmother, Alvina or "Al" as she was called, was a very lovely woman who was always in the kitchen and very affectionate. She was the kind of grandma who wasn't afraid to dig deep into a box of cereal to retrieve the toys or stickers. In fact, she'd stockpile the goodies for months for my brother and me, and when we'd come to visit at their home, we'd run right to the shelf containing all the goods. It was like we'd died and gone to cereal-toy heaven.

Death for my grandfather was one of those things that was always right around the corner. Since his dad had died young, my grandfather thought he was bound for an early grave as well. Therefore, every year after fifty-five became his last year, which meant every Christmas was his "last" because he would be dead by the next Christmas. It became the running joke in the family, and everyone just knew this was Grandpa's "last Christmas." Thankfully, Grandpa had thirty more "last Christmases."

During those visits we got used to my Grandpa's personality. For example, we always knew our cartoon watching was limited because it was only a matter of time before he'd sit down and turn the knob on the TV to *The Lawrence Welk Show*. I also knew that when I'd see him that he'd ask, "Are you married yet?"

One of the most valuable lessons I learned from him is that a man can sew. As a kid, I'd just assumed that it was something only women did. So when I had a little beanbag doll that had a rip on his neck, I found myself asking my mom and grandma to help. But since they were busy, I had to wait. Being a bit impatient, I asked again and again. Finally, my grandpa got tired of me asking and told me he could sew it himself.

I knew better than to argue with my grandfather, so I gave him my beanbag doll. He took a needle and a thread and with those mangled, arthritic hands he sewed my toy back together. At that moment, I learned that boys could do what girls could do.

My grandfather took great pride in saying how things should be done. In many respects it was often his way or the highway. So when my grandma became sick and her health deteriorated more quickly than his, he struggled. He'd always assumed that he was going to die first, but in the end it was my grandmother who passed first. At the funeral, I saw my dad and grandfather cry for the first time. It was an emotional passing for everyone, and my grandfather struggled to understand how it was that he had lived longer than his beloved wife.

I tried to do what I could to console Grandpa Parkinson. I sat on his lap in his wheelchair and hugged and kissed him. I also made a card that had an angel on it and put the card in my grandma's casket for her to take with her. On one level, I knew that she wasn't in her body anymore, but it also seemed comforting to give her something to take to the grave.

It wasn't long after my grandmother's death that I started to have flashes of grief—I would cry because I missed her so much. I was beginning to understand the true weight that the loss of a loved one can create. My grandpa was also dealing with the loss—of a wife he had been married to for over fifty years. Many in our family thought my grandfather would pass within a few weeks or months of my grandmother. However, he lived for over two more years.

After my grandmother's death, I found myself savoring every moment with my loved ones. I was therefore blessed to see Grandpa Parkinson just ten days before he died. My mother, brother, and I were up in Kenmare for a visit; we laughed and joked like always, and we took our last photo of my grandfather. There was no indication that he was close to dying at that time, so we truly enjoyed our time together in what is now a cherished memory.

It seemed like we had only just returned home from that visit when we had to return to attend the funeral. My dad and family made the trip up to Kenmare again. For the second time in my life, I saw my dad cry. With the death of my grandfather, so many in the family shed tears. Grandpa Parkinson lived to be eighty-six years old, outliving his father by thirty-plus years. As he was laid to rest next to my grandma, in the cemetery that overlooks Kenmare, I knew I would miss him greatly.

It saddened me to think that I would not talk to my grandparents again. Yes, I believed that I would see them again in heaven, but waiting seventy or eighty years for that to happen sure seemed like an eternity.

Junior High and High School

As I reflect back on my junior high and high school years, I don't recall any spirit interactions like the one I had when I was five. But my fascination was still there, and curiosity about what happened at death led me to some of my unique choices for reading in high school. While other kids my age were reading *Sports Illustrated* or *Popular Mechanics,* I chose to read books like *Embraced by the Light* by Betty J. Eadie and Dannion Brinkley's *Saved by the Light*. These personal accounts from near-death survivors were fascinating to me, and I was curious to get a glimpse of what the afterlife would be like.

Despite the peace I found in reading these books, my experience in the "real world" was not always as peaceful. Seventh and eighth grades were not my favorite years in school. The transition from elementary school to junior high was a tough one for me, but I found some comfort in those awkward years by getting involved with school plays. Around the same time, I began developing a friendship with a classmate named Doug. Doug was not like the friends I'd had previously, because he was the first kid I knew who didn't believe in God. This was a new concept for me. I had always grown up believing in God and Jesus and the afterlife; Doug, on the other hand, was a freethinker who didn't see proof of God—and thus he didn't believe.

Doug and I had been in a few plays together, and he had invited me to his house to play *Dungeons & Dragons*. He was what people at the time would have called an "alternative kid." On the outside, we were probably more different than we were alike: Doug had long hair, I had short hair; Doug wore a lot of black, I didn't wear any. Doug was a philosopher and freethinker who was interested in the Romance languages, tarot, and rune stones. I was a good Christian boy who attended confirmation at our local church.

Knowing someone with a different belief system created interesting conversations. In the early days of our friendship, I would do everything in my power to try to convince Doug there was a God, and he'd do everything in his power to convince me there wasn't. One might think these differences in beliefs would make Doug my arch-nemesis, but in reality he was one of the most kindhearted people I knew.

My adventures and conversations with Doug were always interesting and unique, and Doug was the first person to introduce me to a New Age bookstore. Although he didn't believe in God, Doug was interested in exploring alternative perspectives and, as a result, we ended up visiting a small shop in Fargo that carried a variety of items including tarot cards, pagan books, and various gemstones. You can about imagine my uncertainty going into the store for the first time. It was said that one of the owners was psychic, so I was even more guarded. Would she read my mind? Was she going to predict some crazy future? But I was pleasantly surprised by my first experience in this New Age world, and learned that it wasn't full of wild-haired gypsies or dark-clothed devil worshipers as the movies had portrayed.

Inspired by Spirit

What I've learned over the years, as a medium, is that inspiration from spirit can be very strong, yet very subtle. Trusting in the communication is the most important part. Growing up in my Lutheran home was a pretty normal experience. My family wasn't fundamentalist, but they were still strong in their faith.

My parents divorced when I was six and both remarried, so I grew up with two families: my mom and step-dad, and my dad and step-mom. Having a blended family enriched my life in so many ways. I went from having one sibling to five, and two extended families to four extended families. Each arm of my extended family had strong bonds, and I have many wonderful memories of holidays and vacations visiting aunts, uncles, cousins, and grandparents.

Thus, when the bond between an aunt and a grandmother became strained due to some misunderstandings, the rift between the two put a damper on the fun family times. I was a bit resigned about the whole thing because, at the time, I didn't think I could do anything about it. I was just seventeen years old and a step-relative; it wasn't my place to get involved. But I soon discovered that when it comes to soul connections, it doesn't matter if you are related by blood or not. As spirits we are all connected, and when inspiration moves you, you better be willing to act. I believe I was inspired by God, given a sign, if you will, on how to help the situation between my Aunt Robyn and Grandma Iris.

Now, God didn't actually outright talk to me, but it was through little things that the big picture was shown. I was sitting in church listening to the sermon, and the pastor mentioned a situation in which two sisters started fighting; this led to them to stop talking to each other. Right away I thought of my aunt and grandma, who were not talking. The sermon also reminded me of the dream I'd had the night before, in which my aunt and grandma reconnected and there were no more misunderstandings.

As I sat in the pew, a feeling started building inside me. I realized that I was being inspired to do something about the situation. I needed to help bring my family together so that they could try to work things out. I couldn't believe the energy and inspiration that were coming so fast and so strong; I had to bite my lip and cheek to stop myself from crying. The church service continued, and with each hymn and each phase of the service my emotions continued to build.

I had never been so moved or so called to do something in my life. The power of the spirit, the Holy Spirit, was palpable. I was inspired to write a letter to the whole family. In the letter, I shared my inspiration with all my relatives and encouraged the family to come together and reconnect.

The response to my letter was a slow one, but the family was appreciative of the gesture. A few months passed, and the healing occurred. Five months after I'd sent out the letter, I received one from my grandma stating that she and my aunt had reconciled. The gratitude and joy I felt was overwhelming; I was so thrilled that my aunt had taken the steps to connect with my grandma, and I was also thrilled that my grandma had allowed the experience in. The family bond was renewed. Two months later, my aunt and grandmother came to my high school graduation party and we took a picture of the three of us together. The dream I'd had about their reconciliation had indeed come true.

I understand now that being a bridge for spirit doesn't always mean you have to speak to a deceased loved one. Stepping into the role of a bridge can also mean sharing moments of divine inspiration with others. And I learned a valuable truth from that experience with my aunt and grandma; I came to understand that it wasn't about getting recognition for helping them, it was about discovering I had the power within my spirit to be a bridge for others. I realized that in trusting my intuition, I could assist people in mending broken bonds. I could become a link, helping them to reunite.

Finding a Soul Mate

When it comes to the soul, there are a lot of theories. What is it? An independent element from God that is created in his likeness but not quite equal? A fragment of God? One with God, part of that magnificent source? (as if God were the ocean and we were each a cup of water). When it comes to soul mates, there are also various perspectives. Some believe that there is no such thing as soul mates and that meeting someone is simply a random occurrence. Others think there is only one soul mate for each of us in this lifetime, and that we better hope to find it or we'll wander aimlessly through life searching for that one true love. There's also the theory that soul mates are plentiful and you'll find different ones at different stages in your life—they may be lovers, they may be friends, or they may be strangers you meet briefly on the street and never see again, but you never forget a connection you shared with them.

I believe I've had multiple soul connections in my life, and I feel extremely blessed to have found one of my soul mates so early in my life. This discovery occurred during my freshman year of college, and was significant to my development as a medium because I had a support system to see me through the journey. Without her, I don't believe my story would have played out like it did. For that I am eternally grateful.

It was the fall of 1996. I was attending my first year of college at Moorhead State University in Moorhead, Minnesota, just across the river from Fargo. I started my freshman year with the intention of transferring to Emerson College in Boston. I couldn't put a finger on why I was so interested in going to Boston, but I had a friend who attended Emerson and I thought it would be a great college to go to. The idea of a new adventure was also exciting. Until I could transfer, I remained an undeclared freshman with an interest in many things, including theater and film production, but ultimately I was at Moorhead State just to take some of my generals and get a jump on college credits while living at home and saving some money.

During my freshman year, I decided to audition for the local community theater production of *Twelfth Night*. I was familiar with Shakespeare and had played Romeo in *Romeo and Juliet* and Claudio in *Much Ado About Nothing*. Both roles were the star-crossed romantic hero who finds love and then faces the hardships. My role in *Twelfth Night* would turn out to be the same—I played Sebastian, a young romantic who falls in love with the beautiful Olivia. As fate would have it, the role of Olivia was played by a woman named Chanda Schnaible.

I'd like to say the moment I set eyes on Chanda I knew that she was the one, but that wasn't the case. It was a connection that was built over time. During the rehearsal process, we started to get to know each other. I learned that she was a college graduate from Minot State University with a degree in communications and theater. She had just moved to Fargo to start a new phase of her life and auditioned for the show to get some Fargo performance experience under her belt. I also learned that she was twenty-three. I was still only eighteen years old. Since she was five years older than I was, I thought I'd never have a chance. I would later learn that when Chanda found out how old I was, she thought, *No way this is happening. He's too young.*

The rehearsal process and production of *Twelfth Night* was very successful, and the friendship between Chanda and I continued to grow. I wasn't keen on the idea of a theater romance because I knew from experience that they didn't last. It was also such a cliché to imagine that because we were lovers on stage we'd be lovers off stage. However, when Chanda asked me if I'd be interested in going to see the Baz Lurman version of *Romeo and Juliet* at the movie theater, I couldn't say no. I picked Chanda up for the movie that night and we had a wonderful evening. She told me how much she enjoyed getting to know me and that she was fascinated by my focus and commitment to creating new opportunities.

On the night of our first date, I put my best chivalrous foot forward by opening doors for her and complimenting her on her appearance, but the one thing she wouldn't let me do was pay for our movie tickets. She said, "You're a poor college student; I've been there. Please let me buy your ticket." My parents had taught me never to argue with a woman, so I let her buy the tickets. The movie was amazing, a visual spectacle, and being Shakespeare fans we couldn't help but love it. After the show I brought her home and thanked her for the wonderful evening. We didn't hug, we didn't kiss. We just said, "See you at tomorrow's performance."

As the production drew to an end, Chanda and I continued to build on our connection. On the evening of our last show, she even gave me a card that said, "I'm begging you to call me...555-7157." I must admit I was a bit numb. Sure, we'd had a great time on our date, but I had been stuck on the idea that I was too young and that she'd never be interested in me romantically. However, I wasn't going to let fear get in the way that evening. I wanted her to know that I too was interested in staying in touch. So I did the only thing I could think of, five minutes before we went on stage for our last performance. As "places" was called, I quickly committed her telephone number to memory. As I walked past her backstage, I leaned over and whispered, "I don't think you'll have to worry about me not calling you...555-7157."

Our courtship continued smashingly from there. We discovered how many strange "coincidences" we had between us. Her mom and my mom both went to beauty school, her dad and my dad both sold insurance. She had actually worked with my cousin at Minot State University. My family used to drive past her house when they went to Kenmare to visit Grandpa and Grandma Parkinson. It seemed like we had all these signs that said we were supposed to be together.

One date turned into four, four dates turned into a relationship, and the next thing we knew, it was six months later and I was accepted into Emerson College in Boston. Chanda and I had built a strong relationship over those six months; we weren't only a couple, we were also best friends. It only made sense for her to join me in Boston—and she did.

chapter

2

A Move to Boston

There are some firsts in your life that you never forget: the first time you rode your bike, your first kiss, your first car. As the move to Boston drew closer, Chanda and I realized that another new first was coming. This was our first big move, and the first time that either of us would be living outside North Dakota, away from our families. We recognized that a new life in a new city would create millions of new "first" experiences. In that excitement, it was comforting to know that we'd have each other on the journey. The plan seemed simple enough: I would move out to Boston to go to Emerson College and get a degree in film production, and Chanda would get work as a nanny for the first year, then apply to graduate school the second year.

Arriving in Boston was magical. There was so much history everywhere, and the energy and hustle and bustle of being in a town with more people than our whole state of North Dakota was exciting. While Chanda lived with the family she was working for, I lived in a thirteen-room boarding house right on the famous Beacon Street in a suburb called Brookline. Brookline is a quaint little city right on the C-line subway. The boarding house was called the Stratton Inn and had been established in 1934. It wasn't kept up very well, but for a college student it was perfect. I did have to share bathrooms and a kitchen with the other tenants, but we all managed to get along together. My apartment's location was perfect—I was just across the street from the supermarket and the laundromat. In fact, I was just a block or so off of Washington Square, a little hub of shops and restaurants with a video store and a pharmacy.

My first year of Emerson was a blur. When you're a transfer student coming into a new college, you have to hit the ground running. I met new friends, was given new opportunities, and managed to create some fun video projects within the first few months. Chanda nannied during the week and we'd see each other on the weekends. By the second year she was also attending Emerson, working on her master's degree in theater education.

The biggest challenge Chanda and I faced during that first year in Boston was missing our families. We did manage to have a visit from my mom and sister-in-law at one point, and had friends visit from New York. We also saw a few familiar faces in the Boston area—I had a high school friend from Fargo who was attending Harvard and Chanda had a cousin living nearby. Having that family bond was important to us; we knew that maintaining a connection to our friends and family was key to maintaining our sanity.

We tried to stay spiritually connected as well. My mom would send me *The Daily Word*, an inspiring Christian devotional, and there were occasional Sundays when I'd get up and go to church rather than sleep in. Finding choices for worship in Boston was not an issue, and the religious diversity was quite refreshing. I lived in a Jewish neighborhood with a strong Hasidic community, there was a Korean Christian church down the street, and Unitarian churches were plentiful. Also, taking a course on Eastern religions was an eye-opening experience for me, a very insightful awakening into other religions and perspectives. Growing up as a Christian kid in North Dakota had imposed some limitations on me when it came to witnessing and experiencing other perspectives and religions; this new awareness enhanced my spiritual journey, and I began to see how all faiths had their place.

The profound inspiration from spirit I had experienced in high school was something I longed for again. It would be inspiring to know that I was on the right path. My desire to find a spiritual connection in Boston was also important because I knew it would provide me comfort in times of stress and be helpful were I to face the death of a family member or friend while away from home. I always had a bit of fear, wondering what would happen if one of my family members died while I was in Boston. How would I get home? Would I be able to go to the funeral? It was not something I dwelled on, just something that sat in the back of my mind. Thankfully, during that first year of school there were no deaths in my family … but Chanda wasn't as lucky.

Death at a Distance

There are certain days in your life that you don't think twice about at the time. However, when you reflect back on that day years later, you see how it played a huge role in who you have become. June 4, 1998, was one of those days for me, and in many respects it was a major turning point in my life. With the first year of Emerson under my belt, I was excited to start the summer.

But unlike the carefree days of vacation in high school, college brought responsibility. I held down three part-time jobs: one at the media center on campus, one at a Mail Boxes, Etc., and one work-study job at the college computer lab. I worked as a lab manager there, which meant I manned the help desk and answered computer questions as best I could. I sat at a desk for four-hour shifts with Internet access at my fingertips.

Although I was not taking any classes, summer school was going on and I was working in the computer lab in the middle of the week, which was a pretty easy task. It was a normal shift, that June day, with just a few questions here and there, so when I received a call from my mom about the death of a family friend, I was a bit surprised. I sat at my desk, a little numb from the news, and tried to find some insight by surfing the web for any information about near-death experiences, heaven, etc. I was not long into my search when the phone rang again. This time it was Chanda, and she informed me that one of her uncles had died unexpectedly.

The news of Chanda's uncle's death hit her hard, since he was only sixty-five years old and one of her favorite uncles. At first they thought the cause was a heart attack, but soon learned it was a brain aneurysm. I tried to console Chanda as best I could over the telephone, and told her that I would come to her as soon as I was finished with work. When we hung up, my desire to find some insight into death and the afterlife continued. I searched for anything and everything on death and dying, life after death, and near-death experiences, and what I read provided some comfort for me. I only hoped that what I found would provide comfort for Chanda.

My research also led me to various websites on mediumship and spirit communication. One website I found intriguing was for a church called the First Spiritual Temple. It was a Christian Spiritualist church, founded in 1883, that combined

Christianity and spirit communication in a wonderful blend that made sense to me. The church had two pastors who were both mediums. Rev. Simeon Stefanidakis was an evidential medium, meaning he could communicate with spirits who were in the afterlife, and Rev. Stephen Fulton was a physical medium, meaning he would go into trance and spirits would speak through him. This all seemed like something out of a movie. My desire to experience such a place was immediate, and I was thrilled to discover that the church was located in Brookline, just a few stops on the train from my home. Most mediums and churches I had run across before were in other parts of the country, but the First Spiritual Temple was in the suburb I lived in. This was a place I could actually visit. At least once I built up the nerve to go.

My research into death, dying, and the afterlife continued throughout the summer. I read more and more about the afterlife, and in my research discovered a new movie coming out that fall. The film was called *What Dreams May Come*, and the minute I saw the trailer on the website, I knew I had to see it. It explored the afterlife and starred Robin Williams and Cuba Gooding, Jr. The tagline hooked me for sure: "After life there is more. The end is just the beginning." It killed me that I would have to wait almost four months for the movie to come out. However, I did discover that it was based on Richard Matheson's book by the same title. I purchased the book immediately and read it from cover to cover.

The novel *What Dreams May Come* transformed my perspective on the afterlife. It was amazing to be able to read an account of what life after death is like. Richard Matheson's description went far beyond my limited images of harps, clouds, and Jesus. According to his book, heaven is a place that we create ourselves. If we want to see Jesus, we will; if we want to see Buddha, we will. Most profound to me was the idea that if we want to burn in hell, we can, not because of a devil but because of our own thoughts. It was also intriguing that Matheson considered his account to be fact, although the characters in the book are fictional. He had researched a number of books in order to write such a full account of the afterlife, and the bibliography at the back of the book proved to be an incredible resource.

When the film came out on October 2, 1998, I saw it on opening night. What a magical experience. The special effects were unbelievable and the glimpse into the afterlife so amazing. As a filmmaker, it was a visual treat to see, and as a fan of the book it was fascinating to witness the adaptation from novel to screen. My interest in all things spiritual increased exponentially after that experience. My desire to connect with the First Spiritual Temple deepened, and I found myself reading as much as I could about the church. My interest in mediumship expanded— I purchased and read *Talking to Heaven* by James Van Praagh, and my dreams at night became very vivid. I would dream about spirit's connection and the peace and love of God. I found that the more I studied, the more I felt a sense of peace. There was a pull, a feeling that something more would come from all of this.

The fall of 1998 was a time of many new discoveries and a quickening of my spiritual journey. I found myself more easily trusting in the flow of things and would not get worked up if things didn't go my way; I knew there was a plan to it all. I recall one instance in which I walked four long blocks through the streets of Boston to get a haircut, only to find that the salon was booked. My frustration about the wasted trip didn't last long, however, because I sensed the reason for my journey would reveal itself as I walked back to campus.

In a few more short steps, I discovered my answer. The reason for my journey was revealed as I turned my head and looked across the street. There in front of me, rising like a monolith, was a bookstore. But it wasn't the bookstore that struck me—it's what the bookstore used to be that stopped me in my tracks. I was standing at the corner of Newbury and Exeter Streets, staring at the original house of worship for the First Spiritual Temple.

Here in the posh shopping district of Newbury Street stood an enormous building, built in 1885 specifically for the study and development of spirit communication. I couldn't help but laugh, thinking about how many people walked by this beautiful building every day with no idea of what it originally was. (I learned later that the First Spiritual Temple moved to a new building in Brookline in 1975, but during its time here, this building also served as a first-run movie house known as the Exeter Street Theatre. The theater was famous worldwide and was known as the Grand Dame of Boston theaters.)

I entered the bookstore, and from the moment I climbed the stairs, my head had a strange buzzing feeling. Being in the building was energizing and familiar in many respects. I knew this was just one more push from spirit to connect me to the First Spiritual Temple.

Time passed; the seeds that were planted during that summer and fall continued to grow. To say that I was like a sponge taking in all of this new insight and knowledge is an understatement—my desire to learn and to understand my spiritual path was expanding. At the time, I felt that near-death experience was the quickest way to understanding, and since I hadn't had one, I wanted to know if there were other ways I could achieve this awareness.

So I created a mission statement for myself. I stated that I was committed to being "a normal individual who can experience the meaning of life without having a near-death experience, a normal individual who can tap into the spiritual world through training and guidance from God and spiritual teachers." Little did I know that this training, and my own development of mediumship, would begin sooner than I thought.

The First Spiritual Temple

Over the years, I've walked into a number of churches. I'd been to various services around North Dakota and Minnesota. I've also visited a lot of churches in Boston. But on the third Sunday of January, 1999, I was about to visit a kind of church that I had never experienced before. It had been seven months and thirteen days since I had stumbled upon the First Spiritual Temple's website. Chanda was working that cool January morning, so I would be visiting the church by myself. As I waited for the subway I thought to myself, "Well, at least it's not as cold as it is in North Dakota."

I boarded the subway car and swiped my pass through the slot, wondering why it had taken me so long to finally visit the church. I had specifically chosen this Sunday to attend because it was a trance service. From what I could understand from the website, during this service one of the pastors would give the sermon in trance. This, I must admit, was a little bit surreal for me. I had never had an experience with a medium before—would this pastor go into a trance and give me a communication from my grandparents? Would this be like the movies? All I could think of was Whoopi Goldberg in *Ghost*, contorting around as the spirits "sat" in her body.

Suddenly I heard a ding and the conductor say in a thick New England accent, "Hawes Street." I quickly popped out of my daydream and exited the subway. As I looked around the neighborhood, it amazed me that I had been so close to this church the whole time. In fact, Hawes Street was one of the last stops above ground for the C-line, before it went below ground on its way to Arlington Street, my stop for Emerson's campus.

As I walked across Beacon Street and down Hawes to Monmouth Street, I realized that whatever occurred at the service, I would just be grateful to have the experience. When I arrived at the address, I found a beautiful, brick, three-story home, which had been converted into a church. It reminded me of the house in the film *Home Alone*. When I entered the church, I was greeted by one of the parishioners and directed to the formal dining room that had been turned into the sanctuary of the church. In fact, the whole main level of the house had been transformed into a working church, complete with a library and a fellowship room.

The congregation was small, and when I sat down I realized I was the youngest person there. I was a little nervous being there by myself and smiled at the thought of what my mother would think. Then the two pastors made their way into the sanctuary. The older of the two was Rev. Stephen Fulton, the church historian and physical medium; the other, Rev. Simeon Stefanidakis, was a kind-looking gentleman of Greek descent who was in his late forties. Both pastors had been with the church since 1977, and they had dedicated their lives to the work of spirit.

The service flowed well. They had prerecorded music for the hymns, and I did have to chuckle to myself because it sounded like something my grandparents would listen to. Since I was used to a contemporary church in Fargo, with a live band, this was a little different. But overall the service was as normal as any other I'd been to—there were hymns and prayers and announcements, offering and communion, too. The whole time, I kept thinking, *Okay, when are they going to talk to the dead?* And since I knew Rev. Fulton was going to be the one giving the trance address, I made sure I kept an eye on him to see how the process worked. When it came time for him to go into a trance he simply closed his eyes, gave a few involuntary twitches, and then made his way up to the podium.

My first thought was *this guy's just closing his eyes and talking*, but as I paid closer attention to what was being said and how his style of speaking shifted, I realized that there had to be more to it. The address given by spirit that morning was inspiring. It touched upon the need to worry less and not take your work home with you—something I could appreciate when the stresses of school became overwhelming. I was a little disappointed, because I had been hoping to receive communication from my grandparents, but that was not the intention of this service. I realized I'd have to have another experience here. I looked at the bulletin to explore other opportunities, and discovered a brochure that would change the course of my life.

It was a simple pamphlet that stated, *The Ayer Institute School for Mediumship: A ten-week class to help you develop mediumship.* The Ayer Institute was the teaching arm of the First Spiritual Temple and was named after the church's founder, Marcellus Seth Ayer. I was amazed that there was actually a course available to help you develop mediumship. I had always assumed mediumship was an ability for the gifted, not something you could learn. I carefully held onto the brochure, knowing this could be my opportunity to expand my spiritual journey.

The Awareness Expands

As I continued to study the afterlife, I found that my awareness of all things spiritual started to grow as well. Chanda and I had never been big into meditation, but found that we were now beginning to incorporate the practice into our lives. In the beginning, we experienced slight shifts in our awareness. There were moments of intense experiences where I felt as though I were floating above my head. I also became aware of my forehead vibrating and feeling energy around my body.

Amazon.com became my best friend during that time, and I found myself drawn to books like Gary Zukav's *The Seat of the Soul* and Dr. Brian Weiss' *Many Lives, Many Masters.* I also was reading more about spirit guides. Growing up, I had heard about guardian angels, and in my new studies I discovered that a spirit guide is an individual in spirit who is with you from birth to death. They are a guiding force who is there to help you on your soul's path. It was exciting to practice techniques to build my connection with my guide.

My spiritual journey with Chanda also expanded as she joined me in the readings. We began to realize that we had been drawn together in this lifetime for a cause that was yet to be realized, and it was exiting each day to explore this new awareness together. Dreams also became a place where I would try to make spirit connections. My experiences were becoming more and more vivid every day, and at night I would request guidance and new awareness through my dream state.

Even though every step forward was an exciting adventure, I found myself getting impatient. I was grateful for all that was happening on my spiritual journey, but the day-in, day-out activities of my college experience were less than fulfilling. I found myself questioning whether I was really happy and committed to my current studies at Emerson.

Thankfully, Chanda was there for me during this time of uncertainty. I told her about my frustrations and my doubts as to whether Emerson was for me. As I entered the winter semester of 1999, I basically determined that this was my make-or-break semester at Emerson. In May, I would decide whether to go back, transfer to another college, or just take some time off. I really wanted to explore my desire to work in a field where I would have one-on-one interactions and make a difference in people's lives. As a result, I began making choices that spoke to who I was, rather than what I thought I needed to do. I made a conscious choice to step away from an extracurricular activity I was involved in on campus that was held on Tuesday evenings, leaving my Tuesday nights open to attend the ten-week Ayer Institute workshop at the First Spiritual Temple. A development class for mediumship...could spirit communication really be something I could learn? It was time to stop asking and see for myself.

Mediumship Development

I must admit I had some reservations before I ultimately made the choice to take the mediumship workshop. This was a new experience for me, and the idea of jumping into something like this was a bit nerve-racking. But I had faith and knew that I had been guided to this experience.

It was Tuesday, February 16, 1999, and the first day of mediumship class had arrived. There was an energy in the air that was invigorating and a sense within me that this could be a turning point. As I rode the subway to the church, I was confident and excited about this experience.

I stepped off the subway car and made my way up the street. As I approached the Temple, I saw a streetlight in front of me and was struck with an idea. I said to myself and my spirit guides in a nonchalant manner, "Okay, if you are here, make the streetlight turn off when I pass underneath it."

My intention was lighthearted and only half serious. I figured it would be easy to pass under a light and have it turn on...you never know when a light has a motion sensor. To have a light turn off, though, would be something to see. As I walked under the light—it turned off. My heart skipped a beat, and I chuckled that it had actually happened. I increased my pace and entered the Temple.

Once inside, I found myself surrounded by ten to fifteen other students, of varying ages. We made our way to the classroom with great anticipation and curiosity. When the class began, we all introduced ourselves and then Rev. Simeon proceeded to explain how the evening would go.

"Welcome, everyone. It's great to have you all here with us. You are about to embark on a wonderful journey. As a medium, you basically stand at the threshold of two rooms. The spirit world is one room and we are in the physical world, which is the other room. You as a medium stand in the doorframe and communicate from one room to the next."

I sat like a sponge, taking in all the information. Rev. Simeon continued with the lecture, educating the students on the basics of communication. "One other element I would like to dispel at our first class is any concern you might have on whether mediumship is the devil's work or not. Well, after almost twenty-five years of working as a medium, I can tell you that this is not satanic. In fact, it's a beautiful gift of the spirit and a wonderful honor to share these heartfelt, inspiring messages from the other side."

After the introduction and an overview of the course, we retired to the sanctuary where chairs had been set up for the class. We all took our seats and observed as Rev. Stephen and Rev. Simeon felt the energy of the group, then moved us around until the energy felt right. When we were set, we began with a prayer; then they asked our spirit guides to be present as well and form a circle around us. I wasn't quite sure if I could feel my spirit guide, but there were elements of light flashes when my eyes were closed, and I had twitching in my forehead and eyes.

As our time in circle drew to an end, Rev. Simeon said, "I have one more exercise before we conclude tonight's circle. I would like you each to envision a table with flowers in front of you. It is a beautiful bouquet with all the possible flowers you could imagine. I want you to picture your spirit guide standing in front of you, reaching out to offer you a flower. What is it that they give you?"

I immediately saw a daisy, and although I wasn't sure if this was "right" or not, I knew that it was important for me to trust my first impression. Later, I discovered that the symbolic meaning of the daisy is innocence, which is often how people had described me.

As I left class that evening, I was happy with how the evening had gone and very excited for the classes to come. Yes, I was hoping for a major revelation or a lightning-strike type of experience, but I also knew that I would take Rev. Simeon's advice. He encouraged everyone to be patient and said that the development of mediumship doesn't happen overnight. I had found my first class very peaceful, and any fears or reservations about my choice disappeared.

The days that followed were filled with reading. I found myself absorbed in my new mediumship textbook, which was written by Rev. Simeon, and I emailed him asking what other books he would suggest. When I'm excited about something I tend to hit the ground running. Rev. Simeon was pleased to hear of my enthusiasm, but he also encouraged me to take it slow. He had seen many students run too quickly in the beginning and find themselves with psychic burnout before they even truly began. I took this to heart, and waited with anticipation for the next class.

Life as a college student is a hectic one. Living off-campus and participating in as many opportunities as I could at Emerson was stressful at times. Running to and from jobs, classes, and home was wearing on me a bit. However, it was my new studies at the First Spiritual Temple that provided relief. Knowing that I would have at least for two hours once a week to devote to developing mediumship was my light at the end of the tunnel.

At the second class of the mediumship workshop, we learned the difference between a medium and a psychic. This topic was intriguing to me, as I had always in some respects lumped the two together. Rev. Simeon explained the difference the following way: "A medium is someone who connects with a spirit on the other side, and a psychic is an individual who connects with you as an individual. All mediums are psychic, but not all psychics are necessarily mediumistic. Over the next few weeks we will be doing psychic exercises to help build your intuition, but the intent of the course is to help you make that connection to spirit as a medium."

Rev. Simeon continued with other aspects of his lecture and then asked for volunteers. "Is there anyone who would like to volunteer for an exercise?"

"I will," I stated. I raised my hand with the speed of a bullet.

Rev. Simeon smiled and said, "Okay, Troy, please come up to the front of the class."

As I made my way up, Rev. Simeon continued, "I'd like you to take a few moments to project your essence to the rest of the class. Now, what do people feel?"

"Love," one student responded.

"Relaxed," announced another.

"Curiosity," responded the final student.

"Good," responded Rev. Simeon. "And how does that relate to you, Troy?" he continued.

"Yeah, that sounds like me … " I said. "Especially that curiosity part."

The class laughed, and I sat down in my seat. Rev. Simeon said, "This gives you the basic idea of how we each have an energy field or aura around us, and how as we open to our psychic abilities we can read the energy off of one another."

From the lecture part of the evening, we moved on to our mediumship development circle and worked on a few exercises to strengthen our intuitive muscle. Rev. Simeon had a number of envelopes with photos in them, and we were asked to take the envelopes and place them in our hands, sensing whether we felt the photo was of a man or a woman, in spirit or alive, and come up with a one-word description of what we felt. The circle varied in its answers—what one person said was male another thought was female, and vice versa. When that envelope came to me I took it and said, "female, body, smile." After we'd gone around the circle once, Rev. Simeon had us do it again. The second time around, I was influenced by others and said, "male, spirit, love." It turned out I was right the first time. The picture contained a member of the church who was smiling. I was learning to trust my initial instincts and not be influenced by others.

In the next exercise, we invited our spirit loved ones to be close. I asked Grandpa Parkinson to be near. It was strange, because every so often I could smell his scent. It caught me off-guard the first time, but it was very comforting. I recalled memories with Grandpa and imagined that I could see him. He looked good—thinner, and he could stand without crutches. Rev. Simeon then asked us to extend our hands and hold our loved one's hands. This part was interesting, because when I first grabbed his hands, they were normal, and then I got a flash of them with arthritis. Within a few moments, I could sense his weight in my hands, and there was a strange energy within my arms. I found this exercise comforting; however, I wasn't overcome with joy or "knowing" for sure. Although my gut told me that Grandpa Parkinson was indeed there, my head wasn't convinced.

The final phase of the circle was a time of messages. Rev. Simeon asked us to stand up if we felt we had a message. I jumped up immediately and spoke to one of my classmates, named Sarah. I "saw" a gentleman in his thirties with short brown hair. That was it. I didn't know if I was just making it up, but I trusted it and gave what I received. It was good to get the first message out, even if it wasn't exactly clear for my classmate.

The process of developing mediumship is a subtle one. I remember that when I started the class I wanted to see spirit as clearly as the chair I was sitting on, only to discover that "seeing" in mediumship is more with the mind's eye than the physical eyes. I would "hear" spirit not as a whisper in my ears, but as a conversation in my head. But it was the physical sensations that I began to literally feel within my body that in some instances stood out the most.

When you develop mediumship, you never forget the first message from spirit that shifts your consciousness and makes you realize there is something to this process that can't be explained logically. My shift occurred during the third class. We had finished our half-hour lecture and were working on the messages in our circle group. A few of the students had shared messages, and I suddenly felt a presence drawing near. It was a young man who wanted to come forward for his sister. I was a bit nervous to bring this information forward, but I knew it was time to share the message. I trusted the process and stood up.

"Heather, I'd like to come to you if I may?" I asked.

"Sure," she responded.

"I'm aware of a young man who is coming forward. He's a good-looking kid with straight teeth and a white surfer T-shirt on. This feels like a sibling connection. Does this sound like someone you would recognize?" I asked.

"Yes, this could be my brother," she said.

I was relieved to hear her recognition, and with her positive response I was flooded with a variety of additional information. One image I saw actually threw me for a curve, but I knew, as my mentors had taught me, that I should give everything I've got no matter how random it may be. They had continuously coached us that we are not to judge the information coming through; we are simply the vessel that passes the information on.

With some hesitation, I said, "Well, I have to tell you, I have a very strange image and I'm not exactly sure what it means, but I'm seeing tortured Barbie dolls."

"What?!" she said with a bit of shock.

"Ah...tortured Barbie dolls, like the hair is pulled out and there is magic marker drawn on the skin—I think that is what I'm seeing."

She laughed and wiped her eyes. "Yes, I can accept that."

As I continued on, I received a few more pieces of information. Then I began to feel a physical sensation in my neck and shoulders. It almost felt like a burning sensation, and I wasn't quite sure what to do with it. My first thought was of an accident, but I was afraid to share the information I was receiving...what if I was wrong? What if that wasn't how he had died? In my moment of fear, I shared what I thought would make sense.

"I'm feeling a warm sensation on my neck and shoulders...I feel like he was out in the sun a lot and got sunburn."

Heather looked a bit perplexed. "I'm not sure about that...but he did die from head and neck injuries, so maybe that was it?"

Of course I immediately kicked myself for not sharing my initial thought, but continued the communication and concluded with his message: "He just wants to let you know that he is okay, and that he looks over you and still has his sense of humor. So the next time you see Barbie dolls, you can think of him."

"Thank you," Heather said.

I sat down, slightly amazed. I had actually made a connection. The images and senses were so clear and yet so subtle. I could see Heather's brother within my mind's eye, and the flash of "tortured" Barbie dolls was so vivid. Then, on top of that, to actually feel with my physical senses the pain in my neck and shoulders. I knew this would be one communication I would never forget.

After that evening of messages, I found myself seeing life from a different perspective. I was seeing more and more clearly with my spiritual eyes and could witness and truly see the God spark, the soul, and the spirit light of those walking around me. This was an amazing experience, and an overwhelming one at that. I discovered that my walks through the Boston Common were not the same as they had been months before. Now I actually took time to pause and view the beauty of every living thing. Whether it was a squirrel running across the grass or two friends sitting on a bench, I could see their shining spirits. The oneness of us all became so apparent. I wasn't seeing white or black, male or female, young or old—I was witnessing their spirit, and their spirit and my spirit were the same. There was now a very deep love within me for all living things.

Returning to class after a successful communication is a daunting experience. You set all these expectations on yourself to do it right once again. I had to keep reminding myself that I was still a student, and this was a place to learn. The development circle opened as usual, and we asked our spirit guides to draw close. Previously, I had had little success in connecting or feeling my guide within the circle. But at this fourth workshop, the experience was different. When I asked my guide to draw close, I suddenly became aware of a presence on my left side. I quickly glanced over my shoulder to see who was standing there. When I saw that there was no one there, I chuckled to myself, realizing that I had just experienced the presence of my guide.

The energy of our circle was a bit slower that evening, and when it came time for messages, we were all encouraged to give one message to someone in the circle. I was a bit nervous. Would spirit be there as strongly as it was last week? Would I be able to communicate anything again? When you are starting out, you face a lot of doubts about whether or not you are doing it right. But the fact is, mediumship is not about "you"—it's about the spirit who is coming forward. I was learning that the best way to make the link is to get out of the way, so that is what I did.

"Hi Karen, may I come to you?" I said as I stood for communication.

"Yes," she said.

"I'm aware of a stocky individual who's coming forward. He has long gray hair and a mustache. He's a fun-loving individual, and when he smiles at me, I can see his crooked teeth. Also, I feel he'd have a few tattoos."

Karen smiled. "Oh, this sounds like someone I would recognize. He's an old friend. Haven't thought of him in years ... whoa."

I continued with the communication. "He acknowledges his party days, and he wasn't afraid to have a few drinks at the bar. He enjoyed his motorcycle and he has a message for you: 'Let the good times roll!'"

Karen laughed out loud and said, "That would be Eddie."

I sat down with a sense of relief. I had passed on the information the way I had received it, and Karen was able to accept it. This made two messages that had connected for people. I still wasn't quite sure where or how I was receiving the information, but I was.

A Great-Grandma Comes to Visit

Before I made the choice to attend the mediumship workshop, I had hoped to have a private reading with Rev. Simeon. This hadn't been possible before I began my studies, so I made sure that I would be able to attend one of the Temple's monthly demonstration nights for spirit communication. "Dem Nights" is what these evenings were called. Rev. Simeon was the main medium, and two students from the graduate class (the next level up) joined him. Together, they would share their messages from spirit with the audience.

As I made my way to the Temple that night, I was facing some frustrations at school and looked forward to gaining a little inspiration. I prayed to God to let me lose my frustrations and enjoy the evening. I asked God to shed a little light on the subject—and a streetlight turned on down the block. This rejuvenated my spirit, and I wondered if streetlights would go on and off near the Temple. When I turned the corner onto Monmouth Street, I noticed that my streetlight was already on, so I asked spirit to turn off the light. It did. Of course, I was always a bit skeptical; I needed further proof, so I asked spirit to turn the light back on again. And it did. As a matter of fact, three different streetlights took turns turning off and on, creating quite a light spectacle. This reassurance and connection to spirit was just what I needed.

Having now studied the process of receiving messages, I was fascinated to observe the messages given that night. Of course, I still was hoping that this evening would be more than just an observation for me; I was hoping to receive a message of my own, but it seemed as though it was not my night—every message was delivered to someone else. Or so I thought.

It was one of the last messages of the evening. Rev. Simeon pointed to me and said, "Hello Troy. I'd like to come to you, if I may?"

I smiled from ear to ear and eagerly responded, "Yes, please."

Rev. Simeon then said, "I'm aware of an older woman coming forward."

Before he'd even finished his first sentence, I was immediately hoping it was Grandma Parkinson. But as Rev. Simeon continued, I became aware that it was not the grandma I was expecting.

"This woman says she connects with your mother's side of the family. She was an older woman with gray hair that sometimes was straggly. She had some bushy eyebrows, and she wore glasses. Her glasses would become smudgy with oil, and then she wondered why she couldn't see. So someone would say, 'Ma, why don't you wipe those glasses.'"

I sat there, perplexed, trying to figure out who this woman was and how she was connected to me. The only person I thought it might be was my great-grand-mother, but I didn't really know her since I was only an infant when she died.

Rev. Simeon added, "She walked with a cane and on occasion a walker, which she preferred less because it was more obvious. She is excited to know you're exploring mediumship; apparently she was sensitive in her time but no one would know about it because it wasn't spoken of. She also lost weight in her cheeks," Rev. Simeon stated, pushing his own cheeks in to repre-sent what he was seeing.

Then Rev. Simeon stopped and asked, "Does this sound like someone you'd recognize?"

I felt a little bad saying it, but I had to respond, "I'm not sure. I'll have to check."

"Fair enough ... " he responded. "However, she says that you should check with your mother, because your mom will have her pearl necklace in her possession."

My immediate thought was: How was I going to bring this up to my mother? She'd think I was in a cult, I was sure. But the communication was not finished—Rev. Simeon brought forward another spirit.

"I'm also aware of another female spirit here. How-ever, this spirit is not someone you knew in the physical world. She is one of the teachers who assists you with your mediumship. She has short hair and is wearing spiritual dress. She stands between two pillars and, in her time, she was one to whom other people came for spiritual advice. She wants you to know that the door to this world is open now, and it will be for eternity. Your family member and this spiritual teacher are working together and are excited to have this opportunity."

I thanked Rev. Simeon for his message and tried to digest and remember the experience. A woman on my mother's side? How was I going to bring this up to my mom? As I rode the train home, it struck me that a safe way to share the message with my mother was to tell her that I'd had a dream.

"Hello, Mom, it's Troy."

"Hi, honey, how are you?" she responded.

We made a little small talk, and then I eased into the communication as nonchalantly as I could.

"Mom, I think I had a dream last night about Great-Grandma Gammy..." I stated. And then I gave her the same description that Rev. Simeon had given to me.

My mother said, "Well, that sounds kind of like her, although a few points I'm not quite sure I remember."

"Well, did Gammy ever have a pearl necklace?"

"Oh, yes, I wore it to your brother's wedding." I could tell that my mom was smiling, but I went silent.

"Troy, are you there?"

"Ah, yes, sorry... thanks for sharing," I concluded.

When I got off the phone, I was a bit shell-shocked. What amazed me most about the spirit communication was the fact that I hadn't been aware of these things about my great-grandmother before, so I knew that Rev. Simeon wasn't somehow reading me psychically. In fact, if he had been reading me psychically, he would have brought forward communications from

Grandpa or Grandma Parkinson. Of course, I also knew better than to think he would do that, since I'd been studying with him for a few months now, but the skeptical side of me was still trying to figure out how it all worked. But the necklace connected, and I realized that this experience marked a new step in my journey.

. . .

Over the next few weeks, as our workshop sessions drew to an end, I had mixed emotions. I had originally taken the course with hopes of hearing from my own grandparents, and I was a little disappointed to not have received profound communication from them. However, what surprised me about the course was my discovery that mediumship is an ability I have within me. This new awareness and connection to spirit was something I intended to continue, and I knew that my next step was the graduate course for mediumship.

The last class of the session also brought my most nerve-racking message. As we went around the circle, I was inspired to go to Rev. Simeon.

> "Rev. Simeon, I'd like to come to you, if I may?"
>
> "Yes, please," Rev. Simeon responded.
>
> "I'm aware of a gentleman who's coming forward for you. I sense that he'd move his hand through his hair like this," I said as I demonstrated the gesture. "This gentleman is also telling me that he was not family, but a neighbor or family friend."
>
> "Okay, this makes sense to me," Rev. Simeon stated.
>
> "He tells me he was about my height and . . . wait, all of a sudden I have the song 'Jimmy Crack Corn' playing through my head," I concluded with some confusion.
>
> "Very interesting," Rev. Simeon said. "This gentleman's name was James, but people called him Jim."

I was relieved to know that the song could make a connection, and I continued. "He tells me that he liked kids, and I see this image of him throwing a football around, although he says that really didn't interest you."

Rev. Simeon smiled at that statement.

"His message to you is one of support. He says he's proud of you because you followed your heart."

When I sat down, I was still shaking. It had been a successful reading, again, and this time to my mentor, Rev. Simeon. Also, receiving the name of the spirit through a song was an experience I would hold on to.

As we chatted after class, Rev. Simeon paid me a nice compliment. "You know, Troy, it's a shame you aren't from this area, because you have the gift and I believe you would be great at public demonstrations."

I was flattered. It was very encouraging to hear that he saw that potential in me. The workshop had ended, and new possibilities awaited around the corner.

• • •

In the ten-week course I'd just completed, we'd studied evidential mediumship—communicating mentally with spirits in the afterlife. All of the students who had taken that workshop were now offered a one-session bonus class on physical mediumship. As mentioned earlier, in physical mediumship one goes into a trance; spirit energies work through the medium and physical phenomenon can occur. So, two weeks after our last class together, we returned to the Temple for this very special night.

The evening started off differently than our previous ten classes. Rather than having our lecture and circle in the sanctuary, we went directly to the fellowship room, where we saw that two round tables had been set up. Rev. Simeon and Rev. Stephen were directing people to certain tables. Everyone was excited, but on some level I believed we all hoped to be at Rev. Stephen's table. He was the seasoned physical medium, so if we were going to experience anything, we knew it would be with him.

"Tonight we are going to work with something called 'table tilting,'" Rev. Simeon stated. "We are going to need you to keep your energy high and have fun with this. Spirit utilizes your energy to help make the tables move."

Move tables with spirits' power. This is going to be a blast! I thought.

I was thrilled to be sitting at Rev. Stephen's table. However, before we even began, Rev. Stephen said, "Troy, I think we'll have you move to the other table."

"Yes, I agree with you. It will help balance the energy," Rev. Simeon chimed in.

"Okay," I said sheepishly, trying not to reveal my disappointment.

I moved to the other table and the evening began. Both groups were focusing their energies into the table. Essentially, we were building our telekinetic energy, and the tables were supposed to sway and tilt. I sat at a table with five of my classmates, and we focused our energy into the table. Nothing happened. We focused some more. Nothing happened.

Our friends at the other table, however, were having great success. The table was shifting and moving, and they were laughing with excitement. Back at our table, we focused harder … still nothing. Eventually, Rev. Stephen realized he would need to assist our table in building its energy. He had an idea.

"Troy, come over here," he said.

"You bet!" I was at the other table in a flash.

"Here, you take my spot. I'm going to try and help the other table."

"Okay," I said.

It wasn't quite what I had in mind, and I'm sure my new table-mates were less than thrilled to have Rev. Stephen leave them.

But in my new location, I could feel the table move a bit. And there was a subtle difference in its movement when spirit was present. It was the difference between feeling like it was just us, telekinetically pushing the table, and the table floating on air. It was almost like the floor was a big air-hockey table, and our table was the puck.

As the two tables readjusted to the new energies, the table I was at now seemed to slow down, and the table I had been at before was going like crazy. My classmates were laughing and screaming as their table started bucking like a horse. It was so active that it eventually broke. This became a blessing in disguise, since Rev. Stephen and his new table had to mix with ours and we now were all working on the same table.

When the table moved due to our telekinetic energy, it was fast and random. When spirit was present, the table moved in a more fluid and controlled way. It was truly an amazing experience. We asked *Yes* or *No* questions, and spirit answered by using the table. Left meant *no* and right meant *yes*. We even discovered that spirit has a sense of humor, because I asked, "Spirit, are you still there?" Spirit answered, *No.* We all laughed, and the table "laughed" too, shaking back and forth.

For me, the most exciting part of the evening came when the table moved in my direction.

Rev. Stephen said, "Ask if the spirit is for you, Troy."

"Okay," I responded nervously. "Spirit, are you here for me?"

The table moved to the right: *Yes.*

I continued. "Are you male or female?"

No answer.

"Are you one of my grandmothers?" I asked.

No answer.

I tried again. "Are you one of my grandpas?"

The table moved to the right again: *Yes*.

The energy in the room was remarkable, and my anticipation and excitement about connecting with my grandfather was overwhelming.

Without missing a beat, I said, "Spirit, are you Grandpa Leonard?"

The table turned to the right: *Yes*.

I began to cry; tears rolled down my face. It had been almost ten years since my grandfather had passed away, and here I was in a small church in Boston connecting with his energy again. The joy was overwhelming and I rattled off many questions, so quickly that Rev. Stephen said, "Slow down, Troy, and remember to only ask 'yes' or 'no' questions."

I collected my thoughts, took a breath, and asked the question that had been in my mind for some time.

"Grandpa, have you been trying to reach me for a while?"

The table tilted to the right again, and I felt his *Yes*.

I knew my window of communication was coming to an end, so I quickly said, "Thank you for coming, Grandpa. I love you … and make sure you tell Grandma, 'Hi from TroyBoy.'"

The table tilted: *Yes*. Then it rocked back and forth like it would if an elevated train were passing by or if there were a small earthquake.

"That symbolizes a hug," Rev. Stephen explained.

Words cannot describe the magic and miracle of that experience. On one hand, I had to laugh, because I never thought I'd be crying over a table that moved. But it wasn't just a table moving—the energy and the experience was my grandfather. Having the opportunity to talk to him, even if for a brief moment, was amazing. It was the moment I had been waiting ten weeks for, in my class, and ten years for, since his passing.

An Uncle's Message

Spring rolled into summer and summer into fall. My studies and my journey as a medium continued. I enrolled in the graduate class for mediumship development at the First Spiritual Temple, and also started on my senior project at Emerson. I planned to produce a short documentary film on mediumship, entitled *Contacting the Beyond*. It would be the first time I blended my two worlds together, as a filmmaker and medium. I loved the idea that I could help educate people about mediumship through film. Of course, it was humorous to try to explain to my crew what they'd be shooting. Seeing my cameraman's face as he went to videotape a circle or a private mediumship reading was priceless.

During this active study of spirit communication, I also began to share my journey into mediumship with my family. I was pleasantly surprised to discover that my dad, mom, and brother were interested in what I was up to. When I went back to North Dakota for holidays and breaks, I had long conversations with them about mediumship and spirit communication. They did have moments of fear, but through it all they saw the positive impact it was having in my life. They supported my study, not only because they saw how happy it made me, but also because they felt drawn to it in their own way and were pleased to hear that their loved ones were okay.

My connection and bond with Chanda was also increasing during this time; it was fun growing together in our spiritual journey. Chanda was hearing about my incredible connections with spirit and became excited to experience them for herself. She joined me for Sunday services at the Temple, and also came with me to a public demonstration of mediumship where Rev. Simeon gave her a message from her great-aunt. She hadn't known this woman, but was amazed when her mom was able to confirm the information Rev. Simeon had shared. Chanda and I also had a private sitting with Rev. Simeon, and we were touched and awed again when loved ones and family members came to share their message.

One message in particular connected with us. It came from Chanda's uncle, the one who had died a year earlier. It was his passing that had catapulted us onto this journey.

"I'm seeing a man come into the light for you, Chanda," Rev. Simeon said, as we sat in the First Spiritual Temple library for our private reading.

"Thank you," Chanda answered.

"He is not a very tall man, a little thinning in the hair, fair skin. He doesn't bring much physical excitement, but he brings with him an emotional excitement. He shows himself in a suit jacket; this is what he would have worn at work. But as he came close, he put on a sweater and says this is family time. Does this make sense?" Rev. Simeon asked.

"Yes, this sounds like my uncle," Chanda said.

Rev. Simeon continued. "I also see with him, a little bit farther back, a desk with books and papers, magazines—he would have read a fair amount. He enjoyed keeping up with what was going on. He stands rather close to you here, and he is reaching out to you to help you with a decision. His words to you are, 'hang in there.'"

"Okay, yes … thank you," Chanda said.

"I'm getting one other element here … Can you understand an image of a horse with this man?" Rev. Simeon asked.

"No, not that I can think of … "

"It was a little bit farther back," Rev. Simeon explained, "but I saw a horse. It was just grazing. Hmmm … you may have to check on that. He now stands, puts his hands on your shoulders, and says, 'I am here.' Also, he's encouraging you to speak with your father."

"Well, that would make sense, because this gentleman is my dad's brother," Chanda said.

As the session came to an end, Chanda and I found peace in receiving the messages. Knowing that her uncle was okay was reassuring for Chanda. The horse reference did confuse her a bit, but she had faith it would become clearer as time went on.

That clarity came just one week later, when she had a conversation about her uncle with one of her relatives. She didn't come right out and say we had seen a medium, because she wasn't quite sure how her relative would respond, and she kept her questions part of the general conversation. But the details of the communication from Rev. Simeon were confirmed, and just as their conversation was coming to an end, the horse reference was also validated. Chanda had actually forgotten to ask about it, but it came up in the conversation on its own. Apparently, her uncle's family once had a horse, but had to get rid of it due to allergies.

Chanda was thrilled to learn that the horse actually did connect. Rev. Simeon had been so nonchalant in his mention of the horse, but it suddenly became the most amazing piece of evidence that this was truly Chanda's uncle. Here was yet another example of how information or evidence that didn't make sense to us in the moment would later be confirmed, providing a new sense of anticipation for our journey into mediumship.

Public Demonstration

An old expression says, "There's no time like the present." In most situations I would agree, but when it came time for me to do my first public demonstration of mediumship, I thought the present was too soon.

I had just spent three months in the graduate class, and we were between sessions when I received an email from Rev. Simeon stating that he and Rev. Stephen wanted to have me participate in my first public demonstration—a group experience where forty or fifty people gather to receive messages. I was honored and flattered to receive the email and recalled how, at the end of our ten-week session, Rev. Simeon had expressed interest in seeing me do a public event. Receiving the actual invitation was a bit daunting, but I figured I would have the next three-month session of the graduate course to prepare myself before being thrust out in public.

Or so I thought. The very first night of our next round of classes, Rev. Stephen approached me himself.

"Troy, I believe Rev. Simeon emailed you about giving a few readings at our public demos?"

"Oh, yes, and I'm flattered and honored. I just think I'd like to take the next three months to really practice, and then I think I'll be ready," I said.

"No, we think you're ready now. We'd like you to have your first experience in two weeks, at this month's demo." Rev. Steven smiled at me.

My heart was in my throat. Rev. Stephen had spoken, and now it was law. I would be sharing messages at the next public demo.

When the Wednesday evening public demo arrived, I was nervous. Keeping my mind focused that day at Emerson was a challenge. As I rode the subway home, I kept telling myself, *You can do this. They wouldn't have asked you to get up and share messages if they didn't believe you could do it.* However, no amount of positive affirmations seemed to calm my nerves. I realized that this opportunity could take my work to a different level. This wasn't about giving messages in the comfort of my class; this was giving messages to a big group of strangers.

I was going to be connecting with someone's father, mother, or grandparent. The weighty realization that this process was not something to take half-heartedly, but something to bring a great amount of respect and integrity to, sunk in. This could be the only time these people would experience a medium, the only opportunity their loved one might have to come forward and communicate from the other side. This wasn't a parlor game—these were real people, with real losses.

It was a rainy New England evening when I arrived at the First Spiritual Temple. One of my classmates greeted me at the door and wished me well. I joined Rev. Simeon and another classmate, who would also be giving messages that evening. We all waited in the church kitchen as people began to arrive.

"Now remember, just go out there and be yourself. There's nothing that you as 'Troy' even has to do. You are simply being a channel...allow it to come forward naturally," Rev. Simeon reminded me.

"You'll do great," my classmate added.

"Thanks." I took a deep breath.

"Remember, it's actually a good thing to be nervous before a public event. Even after all these years, I still find myself pacing minutes before we enter the sanctuary," Rev. Simeon assured me.

Then, strains of the Viennese Waltz began playing through the reel-to-reel sound system. The energy was building, and it was just moments before we would enter the sanctuary. As we waited for the music to end, I recalled feeling the presence of an older African American gentleman as I walked through a subway station earlier that day. I'd thanked him for showing himself and said, "If you're coming forward to communicate with someone at tonight's demo, please come back then." I began to wonder if he would show himself again.

When the music finished, we took a deep breath and made our way into the sanctuary. We took seats on either side of the pulpit.

I felt some comfort in knowing that Rev. Simeon would give a few messages first, then my classmate would go, and then me. But as I looked around the room, I slowly became aware of a handful of spirits gathered, including the African American gentleman I'd seen earlier.

When my turn arrived, I stood, as I had in class, and began to give my first message.

"I'd like to come to you, in the back row there," I said.

The man I was pointing at looked a bit confused.

"Yes, you with the dark hair and blue shirt. May I come to you?" I asked.

"Yes, sure," he responded.

"I'm aware of a grandfather figure here. What's interesting to me is that I was actually aware of him earlier today, so this tells me that he wanted to make sure he was early. He's about five foot eight or so and has a bit of a round belly. He has a big smile and wears a pair of khaki slacks and a short-sleeved shirt. Does this sound like someone you would recognize?" I asked.

"Yes, it does sound like my grandfather," he said with a bit of surprise.

"Well, he's here today to let you know that you didn't show up for nothing. He says you were a bit skeptical of this but that he's glad you came anyway. Lastly, he's watching over you and he says he knows you came here tonight to find out if he is okay ... well, he's telling you that he is. Does that make sense?" I concluded.

"Yes, all of it. Thank you ... it's good to know he's there," the man stated.

I moved on to give two other messages. One was from a very animated uncle for another gentleman, and the last communication was a grandmother for her granddaughter. All the individuals I spoke to were able to recognize their spirits, and I sat down relieved to know that the hardest part was over. I had given my first messages in a public environment, and survived.

The support from my mentors and my fellow classmates was very positive. Chanda was also there that evening, offering me a big hug and flowers at the end. All the support and smiling faces at the event gave me such a sense of security. The evening was truly a privilege to participate in, and I was flattered when Rev. Simeon and Rev. Stephen requested that I participate in all the public demonstrations for the rest of the year. I was now there to represent the graduate school of mediumship development, and it was an honor I took very seriously.

The Transfiguration Circle

As the months went by, I continued to share messages at the Wednesday night events. I also finished my documentary film on mediumship and helped organize a number of "Boston Mediums" conferences, where local mediums from New England would come together to discuss our field and find support and community.

During my last few months in Boston before we returned to North Dakota, I was invited to participate in a small development circle to help Rev. Stephen in his work as a transfiguration medium. Transfiguration is a process in which a physical medium allows spirit energies to work through them, to help manifest a spirit mask over the medium's face with the use of ectoplasm. Yes, it sounds like something right out of the movies, but it was one of the most remarkable things I've ever witnessed.

Dr. Stephen's group met once a month. Over the weeks, we came to see some interesting phenomenon appearing around his face. They weren't complete masks, but some thin ectoplasmic energy would definitely form. In one instance we videotaped the experience, and when we reviewed the tape we could actually see the mask wink. Rev. Stephen's eyes were completely closed, but we could see this very subtle open eye over his closed eye. When it winked, we were all amazed.

Observing and assisting in a transfiguration circle is a slow process. Some days the work is strong, and on other days the energy is not quite there. On one occasion, however, I experienced a communication through Rev. Stephen's transfiguration that I am still trying to comprehend today. As we gathered to help build the energy, Rev. Stephen went into a trance and spirit started to talk through him.

When the time came for spirit to transfigure over Rev. Stephen's face, I had an intuitive feeling that this might be for me. As the energy shifted in the room and the mask began to form, my anticipation grew even more intense. Suddenly, Rev. Stephen shifted in his chair, and his body turned in my direction. Instinctively I asked, "Is this Grandpa Parkinson?"

Rev. Stephen's face smiled, and he raised his hands to wave at me. However, the ectoplasm had formed around his hands, and they were not his own but a gnarled mess of fingers. My grandfather's hands—the same ones I remembered as a boy. There, in front of me for the first time in over ten years, was the physical presence of my grandpa. The whole room gasped and couldn't believe how profound and miraculous the event was.

The impact of this communication is hard to put into words. I'd had brushes with the spirit of my grandfather previously, and the emotion of connecting with him through the table-tilting experience was still fresh. However, seeing his hands shook me to the depths of my soul. My perspective on life, death, and spirit completely shifted. It was like I was a kid again, and all the memories of being with my grandfather flashed before my eyes, making me weep with joy. I was so grateful to once again have my grandfather reach across the threshold between heaven and Earth—to share the universal message that life truly does go on.

Marriage and Preparing to Leave

Our last six months in Boston were a bit hectic to say the least. Not only were Chanda and I preparing to graduate from Emerson, me with my BA in film production and Chanda with her Masters in Theater Education, but we also became engaged and planned a wedding in Boston for one month before graduation. Holding our wedding there was a dream come true, as it allowed many of our friends and family to experience the city we had come to love. It would also provide the opportunity for our families to meet Rev. Simeon and Rev. Stephen and get a small glimpse of our connection with the First Spiritual Temple.

Our relationship with the church had grown beyond just the development circle and workshops. Chanda and I attended Sunday services, and Rev. Simeon and Rev. Stephen had become like family to us. Thus, when it came time to pick a pastor for the wedding, it only made sense to request Rev. Simeon. His mentorship to me and the wealth of knowledge he had provided for our spiritual path had launched us on such a fulfilling journey.

As our family and friends gathered in Boston, it became obvious that there were a few people who were curious to know more about what the pastors (and I) did. In many respects, talking about mediumship was the elephant in the room at our rehearsal dinner—nobody knew how to bring it up in conversation. Thankfully, my dad, who always has a way with words, found a way to break the ice when he gave a little speech.

"I'd like to thank you all for coming tonight, but before I begin I want to share something with you that I just found out. As you know, Troy's always been a bit unique. Most guys, when they get married, have a bachelor party—Troy, on the other hand, had a séance."

Everyone laughed.

"Now, the good news about this séance is that a stripper showed up, like at most bachelor parties. The bad news is that she died in 1922."

That brought the house down! Everyone was belly laughing, and of course they immediately looked at Rev. Simeon and Rev. Stephen to see their reaction—and the pastors were laughing just as hard as everyone else. Needless to say, the rest of the wedding was a breeze.

Chanda and I were married on April 15, 2000, and in May I walked across the stage at the Wang Theater in Boston to accept my diploma from Emerson College. After receiving it, I walked off the stage and into a moving truck (literally), and we began our journey home.

The day before, we'd had our last service at the First Spiritual Temple. It was a bittersweet experience, because we became members of the church at that very last service. It was all a bit disconcerting, leaving the Temple and not knowing how long it would be before we returned. Rev. Simeon shed a few tears, and Rev. Stephen told me, "Spirit is sad to see you go."

Upon leaving, I had no idea whether I would continue my study and work as a medium, but I knew that I would always have a connection to the Temple. This place, and my mentors, had opened up a whole new awareness for me about death, dying, and spirit communication—and for that I was eternally grateful.

3

A Return Home

When Chanda and I returned home to North Dakota, we only intended to stay for the summer. Our ultimate goal was to travel the world, working on cruise ships. The summer promised to be unique for us as a newlywed couple, because Chanda was hired to work at Minot State University's summer stock theater company in Minot, and I would be working as an intern at a video production company in Fargo, five hours away.

Returning to North Dakota after three years in Boston was interesting. The city of Fargo was in the early stages of a downtown revitalization, and there was a transformative energy brewing. I was pleasantly surprised to find a wonderful new yoga studio/artist gallery called the Spirit Room, right in the heart of downtown. The space was great—it had a number of healing practitioner rooms and a large open gallery space for workshops and events. I was committed to figuring out how I might utilize the space.

My experiences with mediumship and living life in a metropolitan city had shifted my perspective on things, and I was excited to share my new experiences and ideas with my friends and family. But despite my overwhelming enthusiasm for my mediumship experience in Boston, I felt in many respects that it was just that—a Boston experience—and that there would be no place to continue studying mediumship in Fargo. I assumed that I would share my connection to spirit with family and friends, and then eventually my development as a medium would fade into the past.

Of course, sharing my experiences with spirit only made those around me want to experience it also. When they asked me to do readings for them, I would often say, "Oh, no … I'm just a student, I still have a lot of training to do before I give messages." I would show them my mediumship documentary film, hoping it would satisfy their need. The only problem was that although the documentary gave a solid overview, it concluded with the statement, "Now it's time to experience communication for yourself." It would then flash to white, and the First Spiritual Temple's contact information would appear on the screen. Since they couldn't just walk down the street to visit the Temple, they would look at me with anticipation, hoping I would facilitate their communication with spirit.

My search for a new church community was also unique. Fargo didn't have a Christian Spiritualist church, so I found myself back at the Lutheran church of my high school years. The services there did inspire me, and I was always thrilled when the sermons talked about how the Holy Spirit is here to inspire and communicate with and through us. Understanding that prophecy, speaking in tongues, and other gifts of the spirit were actually forms of mediumship made it easy to see how these gifts were supported in the Bible. Of course, there were still those who viewed what I had studied as the devil's work, or against God. Of course, that had never been my experience or the experience of anyone I'd ever met.

My enthusiasm for alternative ideas sometimes landed me in unique debates. In one instance, there was a letter written to the editor of our local paper. In the letter, a nun was stating her case that there were no Biblical references that supported reincarnation. So I wrote in as well, citing my references and verses where the Bible *did* support the concept of reincarnation. I was thrilled when the paper actually printed my letter, and humbled when the nun wrote back a very direct letter to the editor "correcting" me on my interpretation. I learned a valuable lesson during that experience ... never take on a nun in a religious debate you are trying to "win," because you won't. Also, it was not for me to try to prove my stance or perspective. I realized my mission was simply to share my perspective, and that it was up to each individual to determine whether they agreed or not.

One thing I had going for me, at that time, was the media. Spirit communication was a hot topic and people wanted to know more about it. Theaters had just seen the huge success of *The Sixth Sense,* and news programs like *48 Hours* and *Dateline NBC* were reporting on real mediums who were connecting with the afterlife. The summer of 2000 also brought the launch of *Crossing Over with John Edward* on the Sci-Fi Channel. People were having more and more opportunities to witness the possibilities of communication.

By August of 2000, after being home for three months, I realized that this aspect of my life—this ability to connect with the other side—was not going away after all. I shared with Chanda my desire to go back to Boston and study mediumship again.

But she kept encouraging me to study here in Fargo and start to share the work with people. I resisted greatly, since I didn't have my mentors in Fargo and didn't have enough experience to do private readings. I gave her any excuse I could find not to do readings.

Chanda knew that I would only listen to my mentors, so she emailed Rev. Simeon, unbeknownst to me, and shared her thoughts on how I should continue my work in Fargo. Rev. Simeon emailed me a short time later, encouraging me to continue my development as a medium. He encouraged me to start by doing small-group readings for two or three people, and also to think about creating a development circle to continue the practice of spirit communication. It was reassuring to hear from Rev. Simeon, and I was touched that Chanda had so much faith in me that she'd called on him to provide me that extra support. The thought of doing a few small-group readings was exciting, but I was still somewhat fearful. I guess you could say I was rather a reluctant medium when it came to starting out on my own, without the security blanket of the First Spiritual Temple.

My official leap back into sharing messages with people came just a few weeks later. It happened in a place I never thought it would, but in many respects it was the most perfect place too start. Chanda and I had traveled up to Kenmare to visit my dad's side of the family. It was a joy to be with everyone, and of course they all had plenty of questions about mediumship, my experiences, and the messages that had come from Grandpa and Grandma Parkinson. I also knew I had to have a sense of humor with the Parkinson side of the family—there was a fair share of kidding around, and more than a few jokes were cracked about what I was doing. As the evening was drawing to a close, one of my aunts asked, "Have you received any messages?"

I, of course, immediately clammed up. It was one thing to share my own experiences with people, but it was another to actually give messages. My aunt had asked the question I'd always dreaded.

I politely responded, "Well, I'm not sensing anything now, and it's hard to give messages to family because I know everyone, which makes it hard to discern what I already know versus actual communication."

Before my aunt could answer, my dad interjected, "Yeah, but Troy, Aunt Joy is not blood-related. She married into the family and you don't have any knowledge of her family background."

As much as I hated to admit it, my dad was right. Earlier in the day both he and Chanda had been coaching me to trust my intuition and share a message if I felt spirit close. However, now that I was right in the moment, I felt fear. My eyes darted back and forth and the sweat began to build as I tried to think of what to say to avoid giving a message.

"You're being stingy!" a voice stated.

I almost responded, until I realized that I was hearing a voice within my head. None of my family said anything. The voice had come from spirit.

"You're being stingy!" the voice repeated.

I then realized that I'd been stingy ever since I returned to Fargo. Here I was, sharing exciting stories about spirit communication, but because of my own fears and worries, I had not allowed spirit to share its message. For the past few months, I had been making the whole thing about me—and now I was seeing that it wasn't about me. It was about sharing those touching messages from spirit, about being a bridge between two worlds and helping families reconnect with their loved ones.

In that moment, everything shifted, and I found myself inspired and connected to spirit like I had been in Boston. This wasn't something that was only possible in Boston. It was something that was possible anywhere. My heart was racing, and I was feeling the same sense of connection and excitement I'd had when doing a public event in Boston.

"Okay, Aunt Joy. I do have a connection for you," I said.

"Oh, wonderful!" she responded.

As I continued to share the communication with my aunt, I realized that I'd made a breakthrough in my development. The spirit barrier that I had somehow created at the Boston city line was now erased. The borders were open, and spirit was ready to flow.

PART TWO

The Messages

chapter

4

The Messages Begin

Mediumship is a process where an individual connects with the afterlife. The communication usually occurs in one of three ways: clairaudience, clairsentience, or clairvoyance (or a combination of all three). When I say that I "see" spirit, I see it within my mind's eye. This is clairvoyance. I often tell people that I see spirit the same way you would imagine Marilyn Monroe standing next to you. You wouldn't see her physically, like the table or chair, but you would see her within your mind's eye.

I also hear spirit telepathically, via clairaudience. I don't hear whispering or an actual voice outside of me; it is more like a conversation that occurs within my head. However, with clairsentience (or "clear sensing"), I actually do physically feel pain or a temperature change within my body. It tends to occur as a twitch or as heat, which indicates that the spirit may have had an injury or an aliment in that area of their body.

When I began to share messages with people in my community, I started with baby steps. I would offer small-group readings (two to three people) in my basement. I eventually made business cards, and my work spread through word of mouth. I had a support group of friends and family, who were open to helping me continue to develop my work as a medium. Dedicated study and a proper circle for development are important, but, like any exercise, the only way to truly build your muscle is to practice, practice, practice.

One of my first sessions was with a friend of my mother's, a woman named Melanie. She had been a friend of our family for years, and when she found out that I was developing as a medium, she was fascinated. It was both comforting and nerve-wracking to sit with Melanie. Although I knew nothing about her family, I did know her, and I hoped she would find the experience worthwhile.

It was a warm summer evening the night Melanie came to my home. We both admitted we were a little nervous, but had faith that whatever was to come forward, would.

"Hi, Melanie. Thanks for coming," I said.

"Oh, this is wonderful. I'm just open to anything," she answered.

"Well, as a medium, I connect with the afterlife. That means I can see spirit, hear spirit, and sense spirit physically within my body. So tonight as I connect with your loved ones, I'm going to bring forward all the information I receive and all I need from you is a 'yes' or 'no' response. Does that make sense?" I asked.

"Yes, thank you."

I took Melanie through a brief visualization and prayer, and we opened ourselves up to receive the communication from spirit.

"As we begin here, Melanie, I am aware of a female coming forward for communication. She is a little shorter than me and rounder. She is a delightful older woman, and she gives me a sense of being connected as a mother or mother-in-law."

Melanie looked at me with a bit of amazement. She smiled and continued to listen.

"This woman tells me she had a way of always being concerned about people. She would have a tendency to mother those around her, particularly a son. Does this make sense to you?" I asked.

"Oh, yes. The woman you are describing sounds exactly like my mother-in-law. And the son she is referring to is my husband," Melanie confirmed.

"She is coming forward to let you know that she is still watching over you all and sending her love," I added.

Melanie dried her eyes at this point. "Oh, thank you, Troy. We all loved her so much, and she is dearly missed by everyone."

"Well, she has one other point for you ... " I said with a bit of confusion. "Now this is strange ... she is making some reference to Psalms. Yes, she is saying that you've highlighted or made a marking in Psalms 139 ... 139? Boy, I'm not sure if there are even that many Psalms. Does that make sense?" I finished, somewhat confused.

"Wow, I don't know. I'll have to check. The only psalm I know of is the 23rd Psalm ... you know, the Lord is my Shepherd."

"Yes, that's the same for me. Well, she just says hold on to that, and if it connects, it will be the way you know she's been watching over you," I concluded.

Melanie left the experience in a state of peace, excited to return home and see if the Psalm connection made sense. I had learned, of course, that specific details like that can take a while to confirm, and I may never know whether it made sense or not. Of course, as a medium I simply give what I get, so it was important for me to not stress too much about whether the communication would be confirmed.

After Melanie's session, I continued my week as usual. My eight-to-five life was in video production, so when our receptionist said I had a phone call, I was not expecting to hear from Melanie.

"Hello, this is Troy," I said.

"Hi Troy, it's Melanie." Before I could even respond, she said, "You can't move!"

I started to chuckle, because Melanie was aware of my desire to travel the world with Chanda, working on cruise ships.

"Troy, you can't move because what you are doing is so wonderful and will help so many people. I don't even know where to begin! I'm so excited," Melanie said.

"What is it? What is it?" I asked.

"Well, I went home after our session to look and see if my Bible had any markings in Psalm 139. It didn't," she began.

"Oh … well, okay." I was a little disappointed. I'd hoped it would be a connection.

"Wait, Troy … the story's not over yet. So, the Bible I normally use didn't have anything, but then I was cleaning my bookshelf at home and came across a Bible I haven't used in a while. I threw it on my bed yesterday afternoon and said to myself that I'd page through it before I went to bed. Well, I was sitting in bed last night flipping through the pages, and there it was—Psalm 139, highlighted in this Bible. I screamed out loud when I saw it. I just about scared my husband to death, since he'd just dozed off."

"Wow, that's really amazing," I said with delight.

"Oh, Troy it's perfect, just perfect. Psalm 139 speaks directly to what I was needing, and the fact that my mother-in-law was able to bring that forward to share with you gives me goose bumps. Thank you, Troy, so much. God bless you and have a wonderful day ... Oh, and don't move!" she concluded.

I hung up with Melanie and sat there, a bit dumbfounded. She had confirmed the information that had come forward. I was humbled and delighted to know that spirit communication could be so clear. It also provided a wonderful example of how spirit is around us in our times of need, continuing to watch over us and provide support.

Energy and Excitement

When people sit with a medium, I always encourage them to come with a level of excitement and enthusiasm. It's natural to be a little nervous for a session, but really, the experience is like a reunion—you feel the same energy and excitement as when you see a family member or friend you haven't talked to in a while. This is the energy to bring to a mediumship session. Your friends and family members are excited to come forward and communicate. Their energy and light is drawn to yours.

Having now sat with people over a number of years, I can sometimes sense people's energies before they even arrive at my home. Tara and Mandy, two friends who came to have a private reading at my home, are some of the best examples of individuals who came with such wonderful energy and excitement. When the doorbell rang, I could already tell it was going to be a delightful session.

"Hi, welcome to my home," I said as the two friends walked in.

"Thank you." They giggled.

"Well, you two are something already. I could feel your energy before you even got to the door," I said.

Both Tara and Mandy started laughing, and I welcomed them into my living room.

"How was it that you found out about my services?" I asked.

"Oh, I picked up your card about three months ago. It's resurfaced a few times, so we felt it was time to connect. I have a—"

"Oh, wait a minute," I interrupted. "Sorry to stop you, but it actually works best if I know nothing about you before we begin. I actually prefer not to know who you want to hear from or any details. Less is better for me."

"Okay, no problem," Mandy said with a smile.

"As we begin here, I want to let you know that wherever you are in this moment is absolutely perfect. So if you are nervous, or uncertain, or somewhat skeptical—or, in your case, excited!—that's just perfect."

They both nodded, and we began the session. After I'd led them through a brief meditation and prayer, I could feel their loved ones drawing close.

"Mandy, I'd like to start with you, if I may. I'm aware of a gentleman coming forward. He's someone I feel falls on the father's side of the family. Now he is standing here, about my height, looking at you with great pride and joy. He's wearing a bomber jacket, and he seems to connect with you more when you were a child than now. Does that make sense?"

"Yes, this sounds like my father. He died when I was five, so yes, he would have only connected to me when I was a child. And the bomber jacket, wow! My sister always told me that when she thinks of Dad, she thinks of him in his bomber jacket," Mandy said.

"Well, your father tells me that he needs you to know that his love is strong for you and your sister, and although he wasn't there for you as you were growing up, he wants to let you know he was watching out for you. He says that he particularly likes to look down during the Easter holiday. He says he loved that time of year and that you two girls looked so cute during those times," I added.

Mandy was touched. "Oh yes, that means the world... Easter was always a big season for us. We'd always get new dresses and take an Easter photo. Knowing that Dad was looking over us during that time is such a relief."

"He gives you his love and wants to let you know that he is also watching over your children, now," I concluded.

As Mandy's communication with her father came to an end, I shifted to Tara. "I'd like to come to you now, Tara."

Tara smirked and said, "Oh, there is someone there for me? I just came for her."

Both Tara and Mandy burst out laughing again and Mandy said quickly, "Oh, don't let her fool you. She's just as curious as I am."

I smiled. "Well, I'm seeing a young woman standing behind you. I feel like she is someone who may have been a friend from your past. She's an average-looking girl with long blond hair and stands a little shorter than I do."

Tara looked a bit confused, and I could tell she was trying to figure out who it was.

I continued. "I see that she is someone who died early in her life. It was heartbreaking to many and I feel a heaviness in my head, almost like I need to fall asleep and I can't wake up again. Does this make sense?"

"No, I'm sorry, it just doesn't ring a bell," Tara said uncertainly.

"She tells me your connection was in high school, and she gives me the name Vicki or Victoria. Does that help?"

"Oh, my God," Tara shouted. You could see the realization come across her face. "Yes, yes, I do know who this is. It's a classmate from high school. I haven't thought of her in years—she committed suicide by taking sleeping pills. And her name was Victoria but she went by Vicki. I feel horrible for not thinking of her."

"She tells you not to worry, she's coming forward to you to let you know that you really made a difference in her life. Even though you weren't the closest of friends, she tells me you made her feel welcomed," I said.

"Yes, she came to our school in ninth grade, and I remember I invited her to eat lunch with our group of friends. We drifted apart as we got into our junior year. This is too crazy—I'm getting goose bumps."

"She also wants you to pass a message on to her mother. She says, 'Tell my mom I'm sorry, I love her, and it wasn't her fault.' Victoria tells me her mom is still alive and you see her now and then. Does that make sense?" I asked.

"Well, it's been a few years, but our paths cross on occasion when I'm home visiting my parents on the holidays. I'll definitely share the message."

Mandy and Tara both sat there in amazement. Despite the heaviness of the message, they both acknowledged the power of the communication and that it was peaceful to know that healing was occurring for everyone involved. As they left, I realized the sacredness of spirit. No matter what occurs on the physical level, when we return to spirit we seek forgiveness: forgiveness for ourselves, forgiveness for our family, and forgiveness for the aspects of our lives where we could have chosen differently.

Through the years, I've connected with a number of spirits who have committed suicide. In some instances, like the story above, I'm actually able to feel how the person died. In other instances, I'm not aware that they took their own life because they choose to come forward in a positive light, showing their families how they were in their best moments, not in their darkest. Most spirits who committed suicide come forward with a deep sense of regret and acknowledge that their choice to kill themselves didn't make their problems go away. They request forgiveness, and acknowledge that their soul's purpose and lessons were cut short on Earth and now have to be played out in spirit.

People often ask me if there is a "limbo" state or a purgatory where suicide victims go. Since each soul is different, there is no one exact answer. What's important to remember is that your loved one is never alone. They are surrounded by their loved ones and guides in spirit, during the minutes leading up to their suicide and the moments directly after their death. Their loved ones and guides are trying to assist them and help them. Yes, there may be some time of "confusion" immediately following their death, but ultimately spirit is there to help them reach the light.

The best thing you can do for those who have committed suicide is to send them your love, healing, and forgiveness. When an individual has reached such a depth of despair that they choose to end it all, the best thing you can do is send love and peace. This positive energy will help them in their spiritual evolution. Of course, each soul's experience is different, but love is the most powerful thought you can send to assist.

A Teacher Becomes a Friend

When I was growing up, there was one teacher who made a huge difference in my life. He was the type of teacher you'd compare to Robin Williams in *Dead Poets Society*. His name was Mr. Lucas, and he was my drama teacher from eighth grade through my sophomore year of high school. Mr. Lucas was a character full of energy. He was a motivator who had just the right words to push you forward. When I returned to Fargo after college, I was fortunate enough to shift my relationship with Mr. Lucas from a teacher-student relationship to friendship. We then reached that crossroads where it no longer made sense for me to call him "Mr. Lucas"; it didn't feel right to call his wife by her first name, but him "Mr." Once we both became comfortable with me calling him Bill, our friendship and connection increased.

Bill was one of those individuals who had his opinion on certain things, but was willing to be open to alternative perspectives. He was raised in Kentucky, then moved to North Dakota to teach. After spending time in Japan on a teachers' exchange program and finding the experience of being immersed in another culture mesmerizing, he had returned to the States with a new respect and interest in Eastern religions.

When I reconnected with Bill, I told him about my new experiences with mediumship and spirit communication. Bill was interested in having a session with me. When the time presented itself, I agreed. I'll admit, I was nervous during the session. Here was my teacher, and the interaction seemed a little backwards... but again, here was someone I'd already known for years, and I knew practically nothing about his family. When you think about it, how often do you ever learn about your teacher's family, or anyone's family for that matter. But with Bill, I immediately became aware of his father.

> "Bill, as I start seeing spirits gather around you, I become aware of an older gentleman who tells me he is your dad," I said.
>
> "Yes, my father is dead," he told me.

"Okay, well, don't say anything else. Let me continue with what he's telling me. He indicates that he was a bit of a gruff individual and would have seen things in black and white. Also, he has a stare that could stop you in your tracks."

Bill laughed at this point and added, "Oh, yeah … that's my dad."

"As he continues to talk with me, I actually have to adjust my posture a bit and sit back in my chair like this." I slid back in my chair, put one leg over the other, and crossed my arms high up on my chest. When I did that, Bill began to get tears in his eyes.

"Wow, the hair is definitely standing up on the back of my neck now." His voice quivered a little. "That is exactly how my dad used to sit."

"Well, your dad is here to tell you that even though he didn't always understand what you were up to, he's proud of you. I do need to tell you that is what I *feel* from him … but he doesn't actually say it with words. Does that make sense?"

"Yes … " Bill said, wiping his eyes. "Thank you."

After the session, Bill shared with me how he and his father had always had a unique relationship. Bill had wanted to become a professional actor, but his dad never quite understood that profession. So, to hear that his dad was proud of him, despite not quite understanding, brought Bill a great sense of peace.

A few months later, Bill and his wife actually began a mediumship development circle. We all worked on making the connection to spirit. Our work together was a turning point for both of us, since suddenly the student had become the teacher. I felt that I was now able to return the "favor" of support and mentoring that Bill had given me for so many years. Our friendship and connection has continued to grow over the years.

A Grandma's Hello

During those first few months back in Fargo, Chanda and I continued to plan and send out resumes with the hope of getting cruise ship work. By the time September rolled around and we still hadn't heard anything, we began getting a little antsy. We wanted to travel so badly and couldn't figure out why it was taking so long. Our attachment to traveling was a strong one, and we were beginning to lose sight of the present moment and why we were still in Fargo. Thankfully, spirit has a way of knocking you on the head to help you see the light. My knock came during a reading with a woman named Rebecca.

When my session began with Rebecca, I knew that it was going to be an emotional one. I could feel excitement, but also emotional energy building, on both this side and the other side.

"Rebecca, as we sit here, I immediately become aware of an older woman on the father's side of the family. I believe this is someone I would place in the grandmother generation. She's a bit of a strong woman and knew how to take care of people. She gives you a smile and tells me it's been a little while since you've seen her."

Tears started to stream down Rebecca's face. "Yes, this is my dad's mom ... the woman you're describing is my grandmother."

"Well, she is excited to be here, although I feel she would never have sat with a medium when she was alive," I added.

Rebecca started laughing. "Well, that's the truth! My grandmother was strong in her religious convictions and wouldn't have done something like this."

I chuckled. "Well, even though she says she wouldn't have done this when she was alive, she wants you to know she's glad to come forward now and say hello ...

Boy, I can also smell wonderful baked goods around her, caramel and cinnamon rolls and such. Makes me hungry."

"Yes, her baking is one of the things I miss the most."

"What also strikes me as interesting, though, is that she keeps showing me this image of you as a younger person. You're on roller skates, skating along her porch and then slamming into the wall." I slapped my hands together to indicate the experience of hitting the wall.

"Oh my God, Troy," she said. "When I was a kid, my grandmother lived on the same farmstead my parents and I did. So every day during the summer I would put my roller skates on and skate over to her house, and yes, I'd bang into the walls to stop myself. I had forgotten about that ... there's no way you'd get that unless it was coming from my grandmother."

"She also has a special message for you tonight, Rebecca," I said. "She wants you to know that although you may be going through some tough times right now, she is watching over you and your daughter. She likes to think of herself as a guardian angel for your little one. And there is a special bond between her and your daughter, yes?"

"Yes, because my daughter's middle name is my grandma's name." Rebecca fought back the tears. She was going through a divorce and had a little daughter who was less than a year old. It was a stressful time for her, and the support she heard from her grandmother was just what was needed.

"The last thing your grandmother tells me is that she needs you to know she's glad you still have the little glass figurines," I added.

"Figurines?" Rebecca was confused.

"Yes, there is some little bird or glass figurine that she says you have, that is hers, or represents her," I said.

"Huh, I can't think of anything like that."

"Well, don't worry about it at this point. Just remember that she mentioned it, and that it is something she wants you to know is her sign," I concluded.

I finished the session with Rebecca and walked her to the door. She was so grateful for the experience and couldn't believe her grandmother had actually come forward.

"Thank you so much, Troy. My grandmother was very special to me and the fact that she is watching over my daughter and me means the world to me. I'll have to think on that figurine. I'm still not quite sure I get it, but..."

And before Rebecca could even finish her thought, the "lightbulb" turned on. "Oh my God...the bluebird!" She hit her forehead. "Of course...I can't believe I didn't think of it before. It's a little glass bluebird she used to have in her home. I have it stored in a box in my closet and totally forgot it was there. I'm going to put it in my living room as soon as I get home. You've provided me with such peace. It's a challenging time right now, and I don't know what I would have done without your message. Thank you for being here and not some other place in the world."

I smiled, and hugged Rebecca as she left.

As I closed the door, I was incredibly humbled by her words. *Thank you for being here and not some other place in the world.* It became clear that I was right where I needed to be. In that moment, my attachment to being somewhere else faded away and I found myself with a new appreciation for where I was. I realized that I was being guided to be a bridge to the afterlife for people in my community. Sure, you could find mediums in New York and L.A., even in Minneapolis. But here in Fargo they weren't so easy to come by. This session proved to be another step forward in my journey toward embracing my role as a medium—in Fargo.

chapter

5

Family Connections

There is an expression I hear now and then that goes, "You can pick your friends, but you can't pick your family." This always strikes me as humorous, and I'm sure we've all had moments in our lives when we've wanted to disconnect from our bloodlines. But the fact of the matter is, no matter what ups and downs we may have had with family members, when they are gone, on some level we miss them. Knowing that we can make a connection with our loved ones can mean the world.

When I sit with groups of people for communication, I have no idea who they want to hear from, or why. In fact, I always give a disclaimer before I begin. I tell people, "I prefer not to know anything about who you are wanting to hear from. The less I know, the better, as I prefer to just have the communication flow naturally through me."

So it's always amazing to me when the spirits that people want to hear from are actually the ones that come forward. That doesn't always happen, of course, but when it does, it demonstrates the incredible bond between family members.

Hearing from Dad

It was a cold winter night in Minneapolis when I drove to a home for a group session. My father had moved to the Twin Cities when I was in high school, so as I continued to develop my mediumship in Fargo, I also began holding sessions with people in the Twin Cities, four hours away. This particular evening, I connected with a woman named Linda. As I was introduced to her, I immediately became aware of a father figure standing next to her. His energy was very strong, and I knew he would be the first one I would communicate with that evening.

> "Hi Linda, I'd like to come to you, if I may. There is a paternal link coming forward. I feel like this is Dad. He's not the type of guy who sits still, so he's pacing a bit, and I see he has a little more substance than me. He has more meat on his bones … darker hair and a distinct nose … it appears that his sleeves are rolled up," I said.

> Immediately, Linda began to recognize who was coming forward. She wiped her eyes and nodded. "That's my dad … oh my … yes, he was a big man and had a very distinct nose. It was broken and never fixed. And he hated long sleeves, so he always had his shirts rolled up."

> I continued. "He feels to me like he'd be the type to say, 'It's a bitch' that he is not here. He says, 'I could have had a few more years.' His death was early in his life. He

also says that he 'would want a drink too, since you're all drinking wine.'"

Linda laughed. "That's my dad. He drank alcohol, sometimes too much in his short-lived life. He died at the age of fifty. I was only twelve."

I chuckled to myself when I heard her dad's next comment. "Well, he says: 'Hell must have froze over, since I've come to a medium.' He tells me he would have been skeptical of this experience and would have expected crystal balls and beads hanging from the ceiling. All that traditional psychic stuff."

(Over the years, I've found that most people are pleasantly surprised when they meet me. They see that I'm an ordinary guy and that sessions with me are just like having a conversation. No dark rooms, no gypsy wardrobe, no crystal balls. Not that there is anything wrong with that. It's just not my style; and besides, gypsy dresses make my butt look fat.)

"First and foremost," I continued, "he says he's okay and that he's never been healthier. His energy and vitality are fully there. What I can appreciate about him is that he is a straight shooter. Quite frankly, I don't want to screw with him because if I do he'll come and haunt me. I also feel I'd be swearing left and right if I actually was speaking like he did. He needs you to know he wouldn't have the patience to be your angel 24–7, but he does come in and knock the jerks out of the way. When you feel like you're struggling or facing some roadblocks, he's there to help. He references your brothers . . . you have brothers, yes?"

"Yes. My dad was a straight shooter. He swore a lot, so what you are saying is so true. And yes, I do have brothers."

"For your brothers," I continued, "your dad is giving them tough love. For your oldest brother—he is going to laugh and have a lot of curiosity about this—your dad's encouragement is for him to relax a little bit. Life's too short to get all wound up. For the next brother, there is this tough love telling him to just act, just jump. Enough with the thinking about it, there will never be the perfect time, it's time to just do it. He wants to make sure he includes the women, so if you have sisters or sisters-in-law, he's looking out for them too. He needs you to know that he believes in you and wants to tell you that you need to be who you are."

"Thank you so much, Troy," Linda said after the reading. "I can't tell you what an impact this evening has had on me . . . in a positive way. I wasn't sure what to expect before I came here. My father died of a heart attack when I was twelve. My older brothers were twenty and eighteen, and his death had quite an impact on our family. My oldest brother took on the role of my 'father figure' while I finished growing up, along with having a wife and child of his own. My mother—she's still alive and has never remarried—had never worked before, and she had to go to work full time to support me. My eighteen-year-old brother moved out of state and began his life.

"We're a close family now," she continued, "but my brothers have issues. My oldest brother, the one my dad told to relax, is very stressed out by many things, both financially and personally. He's very angry with my dad for leaving us, and he felt that my mother put him in an awkward position with having to help raise me. When you said that my father told my other brother just to act, enough with the thinking about it . . . it was so right on. That brother worries about everything. It takes him forever to make important decisions in his life."

"Well, I'm glad the message made sense. Dad definitely has his opinion, and it's clear he wanted to share it here," I told her.

"I've always believed in spirit," Linda said. "Thanks again, Troy, for all you do. You have a wonderful gift to bring the living from those they've lost. I was a little girl when my father died. I've always wondered if he watched over me ... now I know he does. Thank you."

An Aunt's Message

I've always believed that skepticism is a good thing. Nobody should take anything hook, line, and sinker. Discernment is important, and only the individual who is receiving the communication can decide whether it connects or not. I also tell people that whatever they are feeling in the moment right before a session begins is perfect. If they are excited, nervous, uncertain, or even skeptical, it's a good thing. So when I end up sitting with people who *are* a bit skeptical, it's always interesting to see what does come forward.

There are also times when you can tell by someone's outer appearance that they are skeptical. This was the case when I sat with a woman named Helen. As she sat across from me, she had her arms and legs crossed and, although she was a very pleasant woman, I could tell that she had her doubts.

> "Helen, I have a woman that is coming forward to you. She seems to fall on a peer-to-peer level, which means she would be a cousin, friend, sibling. But she is older than you, so she might be an aunt. But there is a friendly nature to her."
>
> Helen listened as I continued. "There is a great excitement from her and a little bit of curiosity. She's also a bit of an emotional person and I feel a little *verklempt*. I don't know if she's the type of person who would have gone to the salon, but her hair is done, and

she comes forward in a very relaxed way, in a pair of blue jeans and a shirt. I'll stop here a moment and ask, 'Yes' or 'no,' is this someone you'd recognize?"

Helen was looking a bit amazed. "Yes, that sounds like my aunt who just recently died . . . at least, I think so?"

"Well, I don't want you to just think so, I want you to know so. Let me give you a few more pieces of information to see if we can help clarify," I said. "She makes some reference to cleaning and says she doesn't have to do it anymore. She makes a reference to dusting around objects, so when you pick an object up, there is a ring. I feel like I can bare my soul to her and she would just take it all in. She was a great listener and a smart planner; if she comes up with the plan, she knows it will work."

Helen acknowledged the message. "Okay, yes, this is my aunt. She wasn't much of a cleaner so the dust-ing reference makes sense. But more than that, she was someone who could listen, and I'd bared my soul to her on more than one occasion. You know, I came into this skeptical, and now I'm not sure what to think."

"Well, that's okay, just sit with it as it comes. The message that she wants to bring forward is, 'Surprise, I'm here.' She's very excited to come forward. She says she's also grateful for how the two of you connected so well. And she says, 'Don't let her fool you, Helen. You have a big fingerprint.' You really have an impact on people. Sure, you do what you do and people pat you on the back, but what your aunt wants to let you know is that it is worth it. What I find humorous is that she says she's glad she's here, where she is, because if the tables were turned she would have been terrified. At least now, she knows she doesn't have to be afraid."

Helen laughed out loud at that last statement and said, "Oh, that would have been my aunt. This sort of thing would have freaked her out. She'd have loved it, but it still would have been a little weird for her."

When the session was over, Helen walked away excited and perplexed at the same time. She hadn't expected to hear from her aunt, and in fact it wasn't even the person she was thinking about when she arrived. But the message was perfect for her, since while she always felt she made a difference with people, hearing it from her aunt and getting that validation gave her great encouragement.

Cousin Connection

After I sit with people, I always thank them for coming. Not only because I got to meet them, but also because I got to meet their family on the other side. Oftentimes I meet people in spirit that I know I would have enjoyed hanging out with, people that would most likely have been my friends if our paths had crossed when they were alive. When I first met Ann, the woman I was about to give a reading to, I had a sense that she would be a fun person to hang out with. I soon discovered that the spirits who would be visiting us were people I would also enjoy hanging out with.

"Ann, I feel two people who are wanting to come and connect with you. I feel there is a male energy coming forward, a peer connection that feels like a cousin or friend. He has a devilish smile and is sitting back with his arms crossed, watching like *I can't believe this*," I said, leaning back and sitting like the guy.

"There is a bit of cocky confidence in him, but it's charming. He also says that he's left the best for last."

(Ann's message was the last in a group of five people. She had sat patiently for about an hour before I came to her.)

"He also came last because then he didn't have to be on time," I added. I looked at my watch and said, "He says it's still early for him. He can come now, at 8:10 PM, because he knows he can still go out later. Does this sound like a cousin you'd have in spirit?"

"Yes, I have a cousin named John who died recently. He was never on time, and yes, he would have enjoyed going out late," Ann said through her emotion. "This sounds just like him. He was a bit cocky but had a heart of gold."

"He wants to let you know that he is okay," I told her. "He also wants to be a bridge for communication to another woman in spirit. She too feels like a cousin or a sis..." Before I could finish my statement, Ann said, "Yes, that's my cousin too. It's actually John's sister Amy, and I was hoping she'd come forward. Her death has some questions around it, and I'm hoping she'll be able to give me some insight."

"Amy tells me that how she passed is not how people would have wanted her end to occur," I said. "I feel there was something across the throat."

"Yes... yes..." Tara said through tears.

"It was very quick and swift, and she says she didn't feel any pain. It's not something she'd have wanted people to be left with. Who did it and how it all transpired—those pieces are confusing for her. I don't feel it's something she's aware of. But she needs you to know it wasn't her doing. Yes, it might have conveniently looked like it, but it wasn't. What's interesting is that your cousin, John, comes forward again to connect with his sister. He'd need to be the voice piece for her, and she knows that everyone wants to know the details. But she wants people to remember how she was and not how she looked near the end."

Ann took a deep breath and said, "The family is so confused about what happened. She was found with her throat slit, and people don't believe that she did it. It was just such a horrible thing."

"Yes, it was, and she is telling you that regardless of how it happened, she's at peace now. She asks you to remember her how she was in the good times, rather than dwelling on her death. She tells me your moment of absolute certainty on the whys and hows won't come, at least not in a way that would satisfy you here in the physical. So just know that your cousins are together, and they send their love out to the whole family," I concluded.

A look of peace came across Ann's face as she heard that her cousins were together, and they were at peace. Although it was comforting for her to hear from Amy, Ann was still confused about why it had to happen. I relayed to Ann that my work as a medium was not like those on TV. I didn't tend to receive detailed information from spirit on how to solve criminal cases. I was only able to relay the guidance I was receiving from a spiritual perspective.

I informed Ann that, in spirit, there is a broader perspective to the "whys" we ask. Some spirits experience their style of death for karmic reasons, to advance their soul's development. Other spirits recognize, upon entering the afterlife, that their death occurred to help loved ones work through soul lessons on the physical plane. But all deaths are a part of a divine timing, and the spirit messages I've received through the years have indicated that even in the face of sadness and pain, spirit comes forward to show that love and laughter still live on. It's this bond that keeps families connected.

6

Love Never Dies

Finding true love in life is a glorious experience. Being able to find your "soul mate" and spend your lives together is something right out of a storybook or the movies. As a filmmaker, love stories have been something I've always been drawn too. Call me a hopeless romantic, but I've always believed in the power of love; I would consider myself much like the character of Chris in *What Dreams May Come.* When Chris' wife dies and ends up in her own personal hell, Chris risks everything in the afterlife to find her and bring her back. When it comes to my own wife, Chanda, I believe I would do the same thing. Some of the most healing sessions I've held for people are those that connect spouses or partners. The truly magical stories are the ones in which spirit reaches across the veil between heaven and Earth and reminds us that love never dies.

A Husband's Reassurance

When I first received a call from Vicki about scheduling a session, I could tell it was a very important request. Now, that's not to say that all my calls aren't important, but there are people who sit with me out of curiosity and people who sit with me because they have reached their last ounce of hope. Vicki's energy was very heavy, and I knew that whoever would be coming forward when we met would create a profound level of healing for her.

Vicki arrived at my home about two weeks after scheduling the session. She brought her sister, since never having sat with a medium before, she was very anxious about what to expect. As they sat down, I immediately became aware of a male figure that wanted to come forward.

"I'm aware of a man coming forward," I said. "I became aware of him before you arrived. I believe this is someone who would be a spouse or a friend. Funny thing is, I see him pacing around my fireplace, so this indicates to me that he would have had a bit of an anxious nature about this opportunity. He is curious. I hear his laugh, and it is kind of saying, "What the heck is going on?" He is very lovable; there is a roundness to him. He says he's bigger than me. Great smile, rounder face. He also makes some comment about his hair, and how there was something about the way he washed his hair that was a joke between you two."

Vicki and her sister both sat there in amazement. A single tear trickled down her face, and she said, "Yes, this sounds like my husband, Gene. He just died, about four months ago, and I've had such a hard time coping." She then took a deep breath and managed to chuckle. "And his hair ... that was something I always bugged him about. He'd never rinse it enough, and he'd always have soap in it when he got out of the shower."

I continued with the message. "He comes forward with a jovialness and curiosity. He isn't skeptical about this, but he would have made fun of it. He would have been committed to getting things right. He wants to make sure the checklist is checked off. He has a community connection—either a community activity or being involved with other people. He would never acknowledge it, but he had a really big heart. He was a modest individual, is how I get him. I get a sparkle in his eye. He says, 'You can't keep a good man down.' I'm going along and sometimes life throws you a curve ball, like life's a bitch, and he's here, and "smack" he's gone, and he hits the ground running over there. He couldn't sit still in heaven. He got over there and made sure he was active with all the people and committees. He wants to make sure I hit it out of the park. If he is going to do something, he wants to do it a 110 percent. I can't sit still long with him. I stand up, move around, just keep going, going, going. He wants to multitask in this process."

"Yes, that was Gene," Vicki said. "He was the type of guy who couldn't sit still at home. We were always on the move, and yes, he was connected to people because he drove the buses for the tour groups we'd lead."

"He needs you to know that there was no pain and that it was peaceful, that he is free and that he is glad he is no longer burdensome. Suddenly I'm outdoors with him, in a beautiful place like Glacier National Park. He says, 'Wow, it's better than I could have imagined, and a hundred times more fun than I thought.' He says he'd never just want to go up there on the harp and the cloud. He hears you every day, and if he could do anything right now, he'd take me out of the equation and he'd just talk to you by himself."

"Yes, Gene always preferred to keep our business to ourselves. He never quite liked a middle man. No offense," Vicki said.

"None taken," I said with a smile. "He says you want so many signs that he's trying to keep up. He's taking a big sign like a big street sign, and putting a sign on the sign to say, 'here is your sign.' I'm always with you and will always be with you. The signs will continue to show and you'll know, but he says there is a strength within you that is moving forward with this. The signs may come but it may not be until the eleventh hour. There is so much you've been asking—the eternal why, it's not fair, what am I going to do. You're not going to see all of that right now. Allow yourself the grief process. A certain aftershave or smell—keep it around."

"Oh, yes, I need my signs," Vicki told me. "Knowing he's holding a big sign right in front of me is so wonderful. I loved his aftershave, too, and I do keep a bottle around so I can smell him."

"He acknowledges that there may be family members and friends that will be skeptical with this," I continued. "And he says that he'd have been skeptical, too. This is your experience, and let it be what it is for you. For anyone that gives you a hard time, I'll put them straight, he says."

I then turned to Vicki's sister and continued with Gene's message. "He wants to thank you as well for the light, the support and encouragement that will help her at this time. He also thanks you for being here today for validating this experience. Like you're the logical outside observer, and he says something like, 'well, it's good she's here. She'll be good at dissecting the experience.'"

Vicki's sister said, "That's so true. I'm here for Vicki, and to make sure this is legit. I'm really not quite sure what to think about all of this ... this is clearly Gene you're communicating with, and I can't believe it."

"That's okay, just let it sink in," I said. "Gene sends his love to you, Vicki, and wants to let you know he's always with you. The last thing I see is him sitting in front of a TV—he grabs the remote and just flips, flips, flips through the channels and nothing is ever on long enough for him to engage him. There is always something else that is on that is better. This is an indication to me that he's doing the same things he did on Earth in heaven."

"Oh, Gene," Vicki said. "Yes, he never could stop on a channel long enough. It drove me nuts."

When the session was finished, I walked Vicki and her sister to the door. Vicki turned and looked at me. "Troy, your message was so important to me. Knowing that my Gene is okay puts me in such a state of peace. I still miss him to death, but knowing he is around me and giving me signs helps me so much. In fact, this is the thing that has helped me most in my grief process. I'll never forget it. Thank you!"

"The pleasure was all mine. I'm simply the vessel. Gene is the one who came forward clear and strong. I thank him for being the one who could communicate so clearly," I answered.

A Wife's Message of Love

When I hold group sessions, it's safe to say that a majority of people in the audience are women. Their sensitivity and openness is what draws them to the events, I've been told. Therefore, when men come, it is always encouraging. During one of my public events, I became aware of a woman who wanted to come forward to communicate with a gentleman who was sitting in the back of the room.

"I'd like to come forward to you, if I may," I said as I gestured to the man.

"Okay ... " He glanced quickly at the woman he was sitting with and the young girl to his left.

"I'm aware of a woman who wants to connect with you on a peer-to-peer level. I feel she's indicating that she would have been a spouse or friend. She's a naturally beautiful woman who would be excited to come forward and connect with you tonight."

The man continued to listen, without any specific reaction.

"She says this type of communication or event is something that she would have enjoyed coming to when she was alive. It's almost as though she understood the 'new age' conversation. Does this sound like someone you recognize?" I asked.

"Yes, I think so ... " he responded.

"Well, I don't want you to only think so—I'd like you to feel confident in knowing so. She gives me a memory she's hoping will help. She makes a reference to camping and those old-school Jiffy Pop popcorn containers ... she said that was a fun thing to do. Does that make sense?

"Boy, I can't think of anything like that. Now I'm confus ... " But before he could finish, the young girl sitting next to him leaned over and tugged on his shirt. She whispered something to him. "Oh, well, I guess that does connect," he said. "My daughter says this is something she and her mom used to make together. The woman you are talking with used to be my wife."

"Well, your wife is here to let you know her love is still with you and your daughter. Also, she says Happy Birthday. She comments that you just had a birthday—is that correct?"

"Actually, yes! It was just three days ago. Wow!"

"Well, Happy Birthday. Also, she reaches out to you to let you know that it's okay to move on. You're too good of a man to stay single—whoever is next will be a good one."

The gentleman laughed as he put his arm around the woman next to him. "Well, that's good to hear, because the next one is sitting right next to me."

The crowd laughed, and I continued with the message to the daughter. "As for you, your mom wants you to know that she is watching you grow up and you are a great spirit with a lot of things you're up to in this lifetime. She'll be with you every step of the way, so think of her as your guardian angel. She'll also be there to help you connect to the right people in the future."

There was a huge sense of peace that came over the family. Later, they informed me that the information was exactly what they were hoping to hear. It had been tough living without a wife and mother; she'd died a few years earlier of cancer. But knowing she was close and sending her approval from above was just what the family needed to move on.

A Husband's Unique Etiquette

When I sit with individuals for sessions, I have no idea what information will come forward that will make sense for them. I simply open up and allow whoever is there to connect. In one session, I connected with a woman named Cindy—and the message her husband brought forward was something I never thought I'd hear in a communication.

"Hi, Cindy. As I connect with you today, I become aware of a very large man coming forward to you. He's someone who is similar to you in age, and feels like a friend or spouse. Now, when I say he's a large man, I don't necessarily mean overweight, just BIG." I stood up and gestured how much taller he was than me.

Immediately, I could see Cindy's reaction to the message. Her eyes started to tear up and her face was turning red.

I continued. "He acknowledges that he wasn't the most sensitive man, and in fact, he wouldn't have come here today if he was alive. But he knows it took you a little bit of soul searching to come here today, and he's glad you did. Does this sound like someone you would recognize?"

Cindy's voice quivered. "This sounds like my husband, Jack. And yes, I was a bit nervous about coming. I so badly wanted to hear from him, and I was so afraid he wasn't going to come."

"Well, he's definitely here," I told her. Then I said with a smile, "He's such a big guy, with such enormous energy, I couldn't miss him. So I'm glad you recognized him, because I don't think I'd want to get him angry. Although I know he's really just a big softy."

"Yes, that's Jack, all bark and no bite."

"He's here to let you know that his love for you is as strong as he is. And that he's over there checking things out for you. He says he's sorry he's not here, but that you're strong enough to make it on your own."

Cindy fidgeted a bit. I could tell she was trying to make sense of this. "His words are reassuring, but I just have a hard time believing this is all real. If there was some sort of image or message he could give so that I would know it was him ... I think it's him but I want to *know* it's him," she said.

"Okay ... I'll see what else he can tell me," I responded. "He jokes with you that you always were the pushy type."

Cindy cracked a small smile, but waited to hear more.

"What Jack shows me is this ... I'm standing in what I believe is your bedroom, and he sits down on his bed, and then all of a sudden he takes his socks off and says, 'Tell her I had bad sock etiquette. She'll get the sock reference because it's something only she would know. Did he have something goofy about his socks, or did he have bad sock etiquette?" I asked her.

At this piece of information, Cindy let out a big sigh—then a laugh—then tears. "Oh Jack," she said. "Of all the things to show, you show me your socks. You always knew I couldn't stand what you did with them."

I listened, a bit confused. "What did he do with them?"

"Since Jack was such a big individual, he had size fourteen feet. Socks were always a challenge for him to find, and so he tended to wear a pair of socks several days in a row. He'd take them off, hang them over the foot of the bed, and then in the morning he'd put them on upside down. Basically, the heel of the sock would be on the top of his foot, and the dirt from the day before would be in clear view," she explained.

I chuckled at the thought of Jack flipping his socks back and forth. I was amazed that this random image he'd showed me was something that would be so significant to her.

"It was one of those pet peeves that you just deal with in marriage, but it's one of the things that only I would have known about him. Please thank him for coming, and let him know that I love him, that I miss him greatly, and that I'd do anything to have those damn socks back on the bed again."

"I will, but he knows, and he can hear you every day. Even when you talk to him in the car when you think nobody is looking—because if they were looking they'd think you were crazy—he hears you then, too," I said.

"Oh my, he does watch over me!"

"Yes, he does, and always remember that you can talk to him at any time. His love for you is strong," I concluded.

Following the session, Cindy confided in me that she really had had high hopes for the session and that her faith had been challenged greatly with the death of her husband. She couldn't figure out why he would leave her alone, but through the reading she had come to understand that he was okay in spirit and that she did have the strength, herself, to continue on.

Together Again

One of the most common questions I receive from people when they connect with their loved ones is, "Are my family members all together?" Nowhere is this more pressing than when I'm visited by an individual who has lost both parents. When I sat with a woman named Abby, I didn't know who she was hoping to hear from, or what she wanted to gain from her experience. I simply led us through a brief meditation and then began with the communication.

"Abby, as I connect with you, I become aware of a father figure who would like to come forward. He's a thinner man who keeps combing the wave in his hair. He's leaning on the table, like this, and is slender like me. He comes forward with a bit of a smirk, and I do notice that there is something distinct about his nose. He keeps telling me that it's not perfect. One of the last things he tells me is that he's hiding his smoking. Like he wouldn't want you to know he was doing it. Does this sound like someone you'd recognize?"

"Yes, that's my dad," Abby said, as tears welled up in her eyes. "He always combed his hair into that wave. He had a crooked nose and he smoked for years and then quit, but every now and then we'd catch him sneaking a cigarette. The way you stood and leaned up against the table was just like how he did it; I swore I was staring right at him."

"Well, he's coming forward today to let you know that you are not alone! That he is with you and there are others with you as well," I said.

Abby began to cry. "Oh, you don't know how much I needed to hear that. Just the other week, I was saying how alone I felt, and to have Dad come forward to reassure me like that is so helpful."

"Now, I'm aware that Dad has someone else with him. There is another woman here, who I feel there is a maternal link to. The sense is that it's his mother. Or at least he calls her 'mother.' She's a shorthaired woman with glasses, and she's fidgeting with her glasses. The feeling I get is that she had a chain or something so she could hang her glasses around her neck. She has a casual outfit on, not her Sunday best, but still nice. Does this sound like someone you'd recognize?"

"Oh yes, that's my mother," Abby responded.

"Your mother?" I said, perplexed. "But the sense I get is that it's his mother. Or at least, he's calling her mother."

"Well, you're absolutely correct. My father always called my mom 'Mother.' Oh, I'm so glad she's here too."

"Of course," I said with a smile. "They are together, and as mom comes forward, I'm aware that she has a big photo book with her. She wants to share the pictures with everyone. I notice she has white gloves on, too, and her fingers are a bit crooked. She also wants me to look at you, eye to eye, and nod. And then it's like I see your whole family with you, and your mom is looking at each one of you and then nodding."

"Oh, mother," Abby said, a little choked up. "She did love her pictures, and at the end of her life she had everyone's pictures up on the wall in her room. She couldn't talk, so she'd look at every single picture, making eye contact and nodding just like you did. She also wore white gloves all the time because she had a skin problem on her hands. It warms my heart to know they are together."

"They most definitely are, and they want you and the family to know that they are with you always. Also, that they are there with the family that went before them and the family that will come after. Your dad says, 'Tell Abby I'm with Mother, and there is no other place

I'd want to be. I couldn't live without her when I was
alive, and I can't live without her here in heaven," I said.

Abby dabbed at her eyes and let out a big sigh. "Troy, that was
so wonderful. Thank you for sharing this information with me. I
can't tell you how much it's helped me. I've been struggling for
such a long time—I feel like I've been orphaned since their passing, but the sense of peace and healing that comes over me hearing from Mom and Dad is so reassuring. I feel like I can move
forward in life with a new sense of confidence, knowing they are
there and they're together. They did love each other so much, and
it's true my dad couldn't live without my mother. She died first,
and he followed shortly after."

What a reunion it must be when two souls reunite in heaven.
Whether people have been together for fifty years or five days,
when you make that soul connection, a bond is made that lasts a
lifetime. It's reassuring to know that love between people never
dies.

chapter

7

When Children Visit

By far the most challenging and rewarding communications I ever bring forward are the messages that come from children. The parents I've sat with have shared the heartache and pain of losing a child. For most, the experience is indescribable. For the first three years of my work as a medium, I could only try my best to understand what it must be like to be a parent; then, in August of 2003, my wife and I became parents ourselves. When our son Jacob was born, I suddenly experienced an incredible bond with another human being, a bond like I'd never had before. He is the best thing that has happened to my wife and me. The miracles and the laughter we have each day with Jacob are priceless and ever since I've become a father, I've found children's communications with their parents to be one of the most moving experiences there is.

When children die, there are a lot of questions that parents ask. Why did this happen? What happens to their soul? Will they age in spirit? But more than anything, they just want to know that their children are okay and that their souls still live on. Many times the souls of children are so committed to letting their parents know they are okay that they will try more than one way to get their message across.

Adam's Story

One of the best examples of a child's desire to connect with his family came when I connected with a young man in spirit named Adam. I first met Adam when he came forward to his aunt and cousin. But once wasn't enough—his commitment to communicating from the afterlife caused him to come forward again, four months later.

It was a warm April evening when I first met a mother and daughter named Patricia and Tiffany. They were two individuals who had heard about my work as a medium through a friend and scheduled a reading with me. As I sat with the women, I immediately became aware of a young man.

"I'm aware of a fun-loving guy who'd like to come forward. He feels like a family link and connects more to your age," I said to Tiffany. "As he comes forward, he acknowledges 'This is a trip.' He is very laid back and has a contagious laugh. I'm drawn to him immediately and see myself hanging out with this guy at a movie, with him being very friendly and outgoing. Dark hair, very good-looking, shorter hair, similar to mine. He has a darker complexion from being out in the sun; he comes forward in jeans and a T-shirt—white, with a logo—and a hemp-style necklace. Does this sound like someone you'd recognize?"

Patricia and Tiffany looked at each other in amazement. "Yes," Tiffany said. "That sounds exactly like my cousin, Adam. You've described him to a *T*, all the way down to his hemp necklace."

"Well, I'm glad he connects. But he says he wants to make sure he gives you a few more pieces of information so you know for sure. Something tells me he likes being the center of attention."

"Yes, that would be him," Patricia said with a smile.

"He also gives me a sense that he had some congestion problems in the nose—allergies, seasonal allergies, I'm full in the nose. He says at one point that he also hurt his shoulder and neck. Last thing I see is that he is antsy . . . he can't sit still very long and is moving around a bit," I added.

"Those things connect too," Tiffany told me. "His mom told me that he'd once had surgery to clear his sinuses, and he also had a shoulder injury from hockey. Antsy, too, so if he's walking around, you can let him know that we know it's him!"

I continued with a smile. "First of all, he gets a bit emotional, and he's touched to be able to share in this communication. I feel a great amount of love. He wants people to know he lives on, and that the last thing he would have wanted is to have people stop what they're doing. Even at his funeral, he didn't want people to cry, and he says he's not forgotten and that a lot of people know he's there. His legacy definitely lives on."

Patricia and Tiffany were thrilled to hear this communication from Adam. Unbeknownst to me, right after their session Patricia called Adam's parents—her sister Laura and her brother-in-law,

Barry. She told them all the details from the reading. Knowing that Adam had come through was a huge relief for Laura and Barry, and they wanted to have their own experience. Four months later, they traveled to Fargo from their home in Minneapolis to have a session with me.

What I appreciated about meeting with Laura and Barry was that they did not tell me anything about Patricia and Tiffany's communication with Adam. When Barry called to book a session, he did not give me any details about who they wanted to contact or why they wanted to meet. So I did not know they were related to Patricia or Tiffany when I sat down with them. I also had no idea that they were Adam's parents.

It was early August when I sat with Barry and Laura. I was, literally, a brand-new father, my son Jacob having been born only five days earlier. I was excited to meet with the couple and flattered that they would drive four hours to have a session with me. In the early part of the communication, I connected them to Barry's father and Laura's grandmother. But as the reading came to an end, I became aware of one other person.

"I'm aware of a fun-loving guy who would like to come forward. He actually is standing between the two of you. He has dark brown hair, a good-looking kid. He has a great sense of humor, and he thought he was a bit of a lady's man. He's much more relaxed than I am, with shorts and a T-shirt. He has a tropical feel to him—he's the type who would go to a tropical adventure. I could sit and talk to him for hours, as he has that kind of energy. He spins his chair around and sits like this." I moved and sat in the chair like he would have.

"But he's not the type who would sit still for long, since he's taping his feet. He also leans over to me and says, 'I don't know how many times I'm going to have to come to them for them to know I'm here.' So I'm not sure if you've been getting communication from him or have sat with other mediums, but he wants to show up again and say, 'Okay, I'm here.' He also has, like, a big marker board behind him, and he takes the marker and writes in big letters: *I'm okay*. He appears younger now, and he's drawing a connection to my own son and is saying that he was the type of kid everyone liked to pick up and hold. 'Yes' or 'No'—does this person connect with you?" I asked.

Both Barry and Laura had tears in their eyes; they'd recognized their son, Adam, immediately. "Yes," Barry said.

"Now he's showing himself to me in his younger years. He's a cute kid with a happy childhood. Loved to buy stuff in stores, and he reaches out to you both and gives you hugs. Now he actually tells me that I should turn my back and allow you a few moments just to be with him. He says he'd prefer it that way, so I will," I said.

So I turned around and gave Barry and Laura a few moments to be with their son, to project their thoughts and love to him and then to just feel his presence next to them. When I turned back to them, I could feel Adam lean over and tell me one more thing.

"He does want to add one more thing … He says, 'It's time to hit the road, Clark.'"

"Clark?" Barry said, somewhat confused.

"Yeah, he's calling you Clark Griswold, like in the *Vacation* movies, and he's telling you to get the family roadster out and hit the road."

Barry and Laura both laughed out loud, and Barry said, "Yeah, I've been known to have my Clark Griswold moments."

"Well, he leaves you with a great energy, and he says he'll be back. Don't worry. You'll hear from him again, whether through me, another medium, or on your own. He'll always be there to connect with you."

After the session, Barry and Laura informed me that they were so relieved to hear from their son. They also told me that he had come forward a few times before, through other mediums, but the most powerful message had actually come through me four months earlier, when I'd sat with Patricia and Tiffany. Adam was only eighteen when he died. He had been on a canoe trip with some friends, his canoe had tipped over in the freezing water, and he'd drowned. Adam's death was unbearable for Laura and Barry, but being able to connect with Adam's spirit brought them so much peace—just knowing that he was okay and that his personality and sense of humor still existed, as strongly as it had when he was alive.

The death of a child is never an easy thing to understand. Spirit has often shared with me that parents won't truly understand "the reason" for their child's passing until they return to heaven themselves. In the physical world, no explanation can ever fully answer the "whys" a parent may have after losing a child. However, on a spiritual level, I've learned from many children who have communicated with me that they're okay and that their passing was part of a bigger picture. Ultimately, children's messages tend to be ones of peace. And peace is the biggest healer for those who have lost a child.

A Strong-Willed Daughter

People often wonder if there is an instantaneous shift in consciousness for spirits when they transition from the earthly plane to the spiritual plane. They ask if people suddenly become enlightened and have it all handled on the other side. What I share with people, and what my experience has taught me, is that although your loved ones may have a higher level of awareness where they are now, their personality tends to stay they same. And it does tend to be the personality of the spirit that people are most able to recognize.

One personality that stands out for me came from the spirit of a girl named Emma. She was a teenager who had died in a fire and came forward with the same energy and attitude she'd had in life. When she first came forward, I wasn't sure how she connected to Fran, the woman I was sitting with. But it didn't take long before the bond became clear.

"Hi Fran, as I begin to connect with you, I become aware of a delightful young woman who wants to connect. She definitely knew how to have a good time. She comes forward dressed in a pair of jeans and is very comfortable with how she presents herself—she has a Girl Next Door feel to her. She says her hair was bigger, perhaps it's bigger bangs or various stages of her hair. Physically, I feel a burning across my chest, almost like something is eating away my lungs—something that happened to her in this area. Does this sound like someone you would recognize?"

"Yes," Fran replied, "that's my daughter, Emma. She was a beautiful girl with big hair," she added with a laugh. "And she died in a fire, so I immediately knew it was her when you described the burning across your chest and the lung issue."

"Well, she's here now, and she's strong," I said. "She tells me that her funeral was packed and that she was there giving her two cents worth from the other side. She tells me she would have looked at people and said, 'Why is she here? She wasn't my friend.'"

Fran laughed at this statement, too, and shared how there had been a few people at the service who weren't friends with her daughter.

"She tells me that she would have loved the experience of sitting with a medium when she was alive. Ghosts, spirits, and fortunes would have been her sort of thing. She's also one to stir the pot. The image she shows me is like a person literally stirring the pot, and as she puts it, she could have been known as a witch sometimes. Her personality is coming on strong here, and she says she didn't forget her broom! Do these items make sense?"

"Oh yes, all of those things connect with my daughter. She would have loved sitting with a psychic or a medium, and she definitely did have moments when she could be a witch, although I feel what she is trying to say is 'bitch,'" Fran said, smiling.

"The message she wants to bring forward is that she's clearly here and that you can't get rid of her. But she also wants to acknowledge that she gives you other signs and it's important to trust them," I added.

"Oh, thank you, Emma—I so badly needed to hear this," Fran said.

"Emma acknowledges that her death was quite a curve ball and that friends and family are still shell-shocked by the experience. She's coming forward with an overwhelming message that one, she's okay, and two, she's encouraging you to not take things so seriously. Remember to find your laughter."

"I'm trying," Fran said, though it was difficult for her to speak. "But I miss her so much."

"She knows…" Suddenly, Emma chimed in with a louder message. "She stops me a minute, and looks me right in the eyes and tells me that if someone tried to tell her this airy-fairy bullshit when she was alive, she would have given them an earful," I said, a bit embarrassed. "Wow, I don't usually talk like that. I'm sorry," I added.

Fran smiled and said, "Don't worry about it. You nailed my daughter's personality to a *T*. She had a sharp tongue, and she wouldn't have wanted the warm fuzzy answer. It's comforting to know she hasn't changed."

"Well, she seems pretty matter-of-fact to me. So if this is how she was when she was alive, then that is how she still is, here," I said. "And she does give me one last thing, although I feel that I'm saying this with a bit of jest. I feel like she has a list of people and she's saying I hope this person gets this and this person gets theirs. And so there is clearly a sense that even though she sees the big picture from heaven, she still carries around her *this person screwed me* list. Does that make sense?" I asked.

"Oh, yes. Emma had a way of holding grudges," Fran said, wiping her eyes.

"It's important for you to know—Emma wants me to look you straight in the eyes and tell you—that you are not on that list," I said.

Fran burst into tears and sobbed with relief.

"Emma tells me that any remaining baggage you have or any concerns about things left unsaid with her, you can forget about. Her love and support radiates over you, and she wants you to know she's still right by your side," I concluded.

"Thank you, Emma. I was always concerned that she would still be mad at me. She wasn't happy about a few things I'd said near the end, and I always felt incomplete. I'm happy to see now that I don't need to worry about it any more. As long as I'm not on her *screwed me* list, then everything is wonderful." I could see that Fran felt a sense of relief.

Emma's strong personality had created a very strong link for the communication. I was also aware that had I not gotten her communication across clearly, she would have haunted me. I appreciated her sharp tongue and her sense of humor, as did her mother. Sure, Emma still might have had some grudges in the afterlife, but she was on a path of forgiveness—and that was the greatest gift she could give her mother.

The Bird Signs

When our loved ones cross over, one of our natural instincts is to look for a sign from them that their spirit lives on. Sometimes those signs occur in dreams, other times through songs, and even in some instances through animals. When I met with a woman named Karyl, I had no idea who she was hoping to hear from. Nor did I know what powerful signs she had been receiving.

> "Thanks for having me at your home, Karyl. It's a pleasure to sit with you. As I open up for communication, I immediately become aware of a younger gentleman in his twenties. He has a great smile, longer hair, a pair of dark blue jeans, and a T-shirt. Physically, he makes my heart beat fast and loud, so he is making some reference to the beating of his heart. Does this sound like someone you can recognize?"

> "Yes, absolutely. That's my son, Ken. He had a great smile and long hair. He died in his twenties of cancer, but what I can't believe you got was the reference to his heart. After he stopped breathing, his heart kept beating for almost two hours. It was something hospice had never seen before."

"Wow, that's incredible. He's definitely a fighter," I said. "Your son is now looking you in the eye and telling you he's okay, and that he wants you to know that he knows you feel like you got the shitty end of the deal. So even though it's tough for you here, he says that now that he's on the other side, it makes sense to him. There is a sense of communication with him, a dialogue, a strong sense that you still have conversations with him, remembering dates, events. Personally, he says he's communicating with you, and he's wanting to let you know that he feels it, he gets it."

"That's wonderful—because I do talk to him everyday. He was my best friend," Karyl said.

"Well, he definitely tells me that if you were friends with him, you were friends for life. Interesting—he also tells me that you have a book that's going to be written. Yes, he says, 'We were going to write a book together.' Wait—he stops me and says, 'Why is it "were"?' There is a book you are still going to write with him. Does that make sense?" I asked.

"Absolutely. I had a book idea in mind before he passed, and after he passed I always sensed that there would be more, that I would share his story," Karyl told me. "Now, can you ask him about the raven?"

"Well, he tells me it's a sign you've been seeing, and it's not a onetime experience. Does that make sense?"

"I knew it! He's been sending us ravens left and right. I knew it was coming from him. We've had ravens follow us. We've seen them both here and at our summer home. We even had one land and sit on our deck. Here's the picture." Karyl handed me a photo of the bird.

"Boy, that's a big bird," I said.

"Yes, they sure are. Oh, this has been wonderful. This is my son, no doubt, and I'm thrilled to know he's sending signs to us," Karyl said with delight.

Ken confirming the raven as his sign provided Karyl with validation and joy. And it became a powerful connection for me as well, because shortly after that session I, too, began to see ravens. Even years after that session, whenever I see a raven I think of Ken.

A Daughter's Hello

As a medium, I've had the opportunity to share messages with people at a variety of venues. One of my favorite places to offer my services is at holistic or metaphysical expos. Expos are a great place to meet like-minded individuals and connect with a variety of people. At my very first expo, I had a special encounter with a woman named Denise and her mother, Janelle. The mother-daughter team had a booth down the aisle from me, and they'd heard about my work as a medium through a mutual friend. When they found out I was going to be at the expo, they immediately signed up for a session.

Denise, the thirty-something daughter, came for a fifteen-minute session. During the communication, her grandfather came forward, along with one other family member. Denise was pleased by the experience and the ability to connect with her grandfather, but she admitted she was hoping to hear from someone else. This is a natural part of communication; oftentimes people want to hear from a specific person, but for whatever reason I don't connect with that spirit.

In Denise's case, I told her to have faith that the spirit she was hoping to hear from was still around her, and she would receive a message at another time. Denise thanked me and went back to her booth. Shortly after Denise's session, Janelle came over for her own reading. As Janelle sat down with me, I knew that this session was going to be different.

"Hello, Janelle, nice to meet you. How's your day going at your booth?"

"Oh, good, thank you. I know that in most cases you don't have people say anything before you begin, but I can't help myself. I want to hear from Amanda," Janelle told me.

"Amanda, huh? Well, okay—I can't guarantee that I'll be able to connect with the specific spirit you're hoping to hear from, but I'll share with you what I get. Does that sound okay?"

"Yes. Thank you for trying," Janelle said.

"Well, right off the bat, I become aware of a young girl in her teens with a very youthful energy and laughter. She acknowledges that she liked to have fun. This is your granddaughter, yes? This is Denise's daughter, yes?" I suddenly realized that this was the spirit that Denise had hoped to hear from.

"Yes, yes, it is. Oh, I'm so relieved to have her here," Janelle said, visibly moved.

"Amanda admits that she likes to keep everyone on their toes and also that she had a tendency to be a bit dramatic, which is why she was holding out on the communication. She jokes that she wanted to be asked to come forward. It's not that she isn't already around you all, but in this instance she's being like she was on Earth, and she wants to be asked. Does that make sense?"

"Oh, yes," Janelle said with a smile. "Amanda had a tendency to be on the dramatic side sometimes, and yes, as the oldest sister in the family, she always wanted to be asked before someone took something or did something.

She hated it when people just assumed she'd do something."

"She's a beautiful young lady, and I feel a very sudden impact in her passing. Did she die in an accident?" I asked.

"Yes. It was devastating, not only to our family but to the whole community," Janelle said.

"She's an old soul, as I'd call her, and I feel as though she wants to let both you and Denise know how much she loves you and sends support to you both. She also understands her soul's purpose and knows why her mission was complete on Earth. She needs to hit home that she and Denise are already connected, and she keeps saying, 'Hello, Mom!'"

"Denise will be so glad to hear that."

"Amanda tells me two more things. One, she needs you to tell Denise that the hidden gift in her passing is that it will propel Denise on a new journey. This new journey maybe isn't one she wanted to take, meaning Denise would give it all up to have Amanda back, but since Amanda is where she needs to be, it's important for Denise to embrace the road she's on. Denise is a force to be reckoned with, and she will change the world. Will you share that with Denise?"

Janelle nodded through tears of joy and pride.

"The second thing Amanda tells me is she's going to give you and Denise a message as you drive home together. She's going to play a song on the radio, and the lyrics of the song are going to speak to your soul—you'll know it's from her. Now, the funny thing is she tells me it will be on a country station, and she rolls her eyes—I don't sense that she would have normally listened to a country station. Does that make sense?" I asked.

"Oh, Amanda. Yes, yes, that does make sense. Amanda wasn't a big country fan, and if she didn't like something she would roll her eyes," Janelle said. "But I don't know what the song is."

"That's okay, you won't yet. It's just something that you have to wait for when you're driving home. Amanda concludes by thanking you for asking her to come. She sends her love to you and knows that her communication will create a big shift for you and Denise."

After the session, Janelle immediately went to tell Denise what had occurred. Shortly thereafter, Denise came up and thanked me. She'd never thought to come right out and ask Amanda to come, and she laughed because she knew that that was just how Amanda would be.

A few days later, I heard back from Denise, and she told me that Amanda's message to her did come through a song on the country station as they were driving home. When they turned on the radio, they heard the song "Stand" by Rascal Flatts, and the lyrics spoke directly to what Denise had been feeling. Denise thanked me again for the message and was so grateful to know that Amanda was watching her, cheering her on as she prepared to start a new journey in her life. If Amanda told Denise she was going to change the world, Denise knew she better get started.

chapter

8

The Sitter Becomes the Medium

As an evidential medium, my goal during readings is quite simple: bring forward clear, evidential communication from a loved one or family member in such a way that the person I'm sitting with recognizes the spirit and is able to find peace, knowing that death does not exist and our souls live on. As a medium, though, I've come to learn that that's not always how the process works. There are times when spirits do come forward for people, but the person I'm communicating with does not recognize the spirit.

In some of those instances, the person I'm sharing the message with might just have to go and do a little family research; other times it might be an individual that they don't personally know. In the situations where the person doesn't actually know the spirit, I tell them that they may have to share this message or communication with a friend or an acquaintance. Even though they are the sitter, they have now become the medium for the medium. Although the experience of receiving communication from someone you don't know, or don't remember, can be frustrating in the moment, it is amazing when the stories are validated at a later date.

Seeing a Beetle

Most of my individual sessions last an hour. In that time, four to five spirits come forward and share their messages. I was into the third communication with a woman named Wanda when I realized that this was to become one of those sessions where my sitter would have to pass the message on to someone else.

"Okay, Wanda. I'm now aware of another woman who would like to come forward to communicate with you. She acknowledges that she would fall into the peer-to-peer connection, and I'll be honest—the first way that I'm seeing this woman is in a sickly state, very gaunt," I began.

"There is a tiredness that comes to this woman. And a feeling like I'm breathing through water, or there is congestion in my chest. She has to lie down here on this couch first, with a bit of dwindling energy coming from her. She wasn't an old person when she passed away; she would have died when she was younger in years. The initials H.S. or S.H. are related to her and there's a sense of being surrounded by little dogs. I get a sense of strawberry blond hair; she's showing herself healthier and younger in years. Beautiful face, now that she's showing herself as more vibrant than when she was ill. Does this sound like someone you would recognize?"

"No, not at the moment," Wanda responded.

"Okay, well, I also have the sense that this may be a message you may have to pass on to another individual. This spirit tells me there would be a friend or coworker who knew you were coming here tonight and you'll pass this connection on to her. It's an experiment for me and for you. Looks like you'll be the medium for the medium on this one," I joked.

"Okay, well, I'll make sure to take notes," Wanda said.

"It's interesting, because the woman who this will connect to is shorter and round-faced, with glasses—glasses that seem way too big for her face. The connection between the two of them would have been late '70s or early '80s. The person in the physical now would hate to admit she had glasses that big. There is also a 'three' connection to this woman—either she had three children, was born or died on the third...just remember that she acknowledges the 'three.' Lastly, she flashes me the image of an old VW Beetle. Again, something you might not know, but please pass it on. Sometimes the strangest images are the ones that connect the most. Her message to her friend is quite simply 'I'm here and I'm okay,'" I concluded.

"Wow, very interesting. I'm still clueless, but I'll try to pass it on," Wanda told me.

"I guess that's all we can do. But please, let me know if any of this connects," I requested.

"You'll be the first to know," Wanda said with a smile.

I continued with the rest of the communication, and Wanda found the evening to be uplifting. As she left, I hoped that clarity would come about the message from the spirit. Yet I had been in this situation before and oftentimes had not heard back, so in faith I let it be and knew that it would connect when it needed to.

About a week went by, and life continued on as normal. I had actually forgotten about the communication when I received a call from Wanda.

"Hello, Troy?" I heard a voice on the phone say. "This is Wanda from last week."

"Hi Wanda, how are you?"

"Oh, I'm great..." Wanda responded. "Remember bringing forward the sickly woman on the couch?"

Immediately the images from that session came rushing back. "Yes."

"Well, I checked in with the gals that knew of our session, and we have a match for the woman. It turns out to be my coworker's aunt's best friend. Her last name was Stranderhoft. Remember, you referenced the S.H. connection?"

"Oh, yes, that's correct."

"And just like you said, she indeed was a thin, strawberry blond. She died at home of heart disease/heart failure, and the fatigue also made sense. She always had tons of dogs around her. Also, there was the three connection to either children or a date—well, it turns out that she has three children, and she died on the third," she said.

"That's wonderful. I'm so glad to hear that the connection registered!"

"But Troy, the kicker to the whole thing, and I just get goose bumps thinking about it now, is the VW Beetle reference you made..."

"Yes?"

"It wasn't a car—it was her nickname! She went by the nickname Beetle." Wanda was so excited she could hardly catch her breath.

"Wow! She must have known that the only way I'd get the name is if I saw the car," I said with amazement.

"We are all so excited that this message was able to be passed on, and needless to say, my coworker's aunt is ecstatic! Thanks again so much for the reading," Wanda said.

As I hung up the phone, I acknowledged and thanked spirit for the message. As a medium, you may never know how the messages connect, but when you receive the validation, with such detail, that it all made sense, it truly reinforces the magic and the miracle of the spirits' commitment to share their message—that life goes on.

Message at the Mechanic

I often hold small-group events in people's homes, in which people invite their friends and family over for an evening of communication. An evening with a medium is not your usual dinner party, and as a result I usually come to the event with a light-hearted attitude, to make sure everyone is comfortable with what will occur. On one occasion, I was invited to a birthday celebration. The host, Steph, whose birthday it was, wanted all of her friends to have a memorable evening. As we went through the session, I shared various messages with people in the group. One woman heard from her father; another woman heard from her grandmother. When the evening came to an end, there was only one person remaining who hadn't heard anything yet—Steph.

> "Okay, birthday girl, I'd like to come forward with a message for you."
>
> "Excellent!" Steph said.
>
> "There is a young man here who would like to come forward."
>
> "Okay."
>
> "As I see him, he falls into that peer-to-peer connection. He's a good-looking kid in his late teens or early twenties. He comes forward with blond hair and a strong

message. He's kind of a cocky kid, with a great sense of humor—the life of the party to say the least. Does this sound like someone you might be aware of?" I asked.

"I can't think of anyone I know who died at a young age like this," she said, a bit confused.

"Okay, well, he is a persistent individual, and he tells me that you're the type of person who will know how to pass the message on to the person that needs it."

"Absolutely. Tell me more, and I'll happily be the messenger," Steph said with conviction.

I wasn't surprised that Steph was receiving a communication from a spirit she didn't recognize. She had such a contagious energy and a spunk that everyone would immediately feel like her friend.

"Well," I told her, "I'm aware that this young man died in an accident. And I can feel the impact on my right side, in the midsection. I sense he may have had internal bleeding, and the right side of my head feels injured too. He didn't have the chance to say good-bye to people," I said.

"Hmmm, I still can't think of who it is," Steph said uncertainly.

"That's okay. This kid tells me that you'll either meet someone, or someone you visit will know who he is. Give it some time, but it will connect," I concluded.

When the session was over I went on my way, hoping that I hadn't confused the birthday girl too much. She'd been hoping to hear from one of her loved ones, and who came forward but a twenty-something guy she'd never met.

About six months went by before clarity came for Steph. I had actually forgotten about the communication, so when Steph called I wasn't thinking about it.

"Hi Troy, it's Steph."

"Oh hi, Steph, how are you?" Steph and I had actually stayed in contact, about other things, since our session.

"Troy, do you remember the reading you gave me on my birthday?"

"Boy, I'm sorry, I don't right at the moment—a lot of times I don't recall the communications. I connect with so many people that oftentimes it just flows through. So forgive me, but refresh my memory," I said.

"Well, you brought forward a young man in his late teens who died from a vehicle accident. He didn't know me but he wanted me to pass the message on. Does that ring a bell?"

"Oh, yeah…now it's coming back. He had some injury to his head, and there was internal bleeding or something," I said vaguely.

"Yes, yes, that's the one!" Steph responded with excitement. "So the other day, I took my car into the mechanic. As I sat down to wait, I noticed that my mechanic, Mike, had a cool, shrine-like display in the lobby. So I commented about it."

"Hey, Mike, that's a cool shrine."
"Yeah, I made it in remembrance of my brother."
"Oh, I'm so sorry. But what a cool way to remember him."

"At that moment," Steph continued, "I didn't even think about the young guy from our session, because I thought Mike only had older brothers."

Mike said, "Yeah, it's coming up on a year now, and it's been really hard on me because he was so young."
"Young? I thought you only had older brothers."
"I do, but I also had a cousin who was like a younger brother to me. He lived with us since he was five years old, so he's always been my younger brother."

"He didn't happen to be in his late teens, did he? With blond hair and kind of a cocky but fun-loving personality?" Steph said, feeling a little reservation.

"Yes, why?" Mike sounded shocked.

"Umm, Mike, what I'm about to say to you may not make sense right away, but I just want you to take it in."

"Okay!?! What are you going to tell me?"

"Well, on my birthday, my girlfriends and I got together, and I wanted to do something a little different. So I had this medium named Troy come to my house, and he brought forward the spirit of a young man in his late teens who was a cocky kid but had a sense of humor. He was the life of the party, but unfortunately he died in a car accident. Troy said the guy had an injury to the right side of his head and some internal bleeding. Did your brother die in a car accident?"

Mike was shaking now, leaning back on the counter and getting a little choked up. *"Oh, my God, how can this be? My brother was nineteen, he was the life of the party, and he did die in a car accident. He was thrown from the car and had injuries on the right side of his body, including his head, but what he ultimately died from was his internal bleeding. How can you know this, Steph? How can this Troy know this? I don't like this—this is freaking me out."*

"I know it's strange," Steph told him. *"I can't figure out how it's happening either, but your brother came to me six months ago, knowing that I would pass the message on to you now. I don't understand it, but he needs you to know that he is okay! He needs you to know his spirit lives on!"*

As Steph told me the story, I couldn't believe what I was hearing. I had never had a communication passed on in such a way. Steph then told me, "Troy, I get chills talking about it now. Mike was a bit shell-shocked, but he did find some peace in knowing his brother was okay. He also said he'd never believed in this stuff before, but this experience has changed his mind. Can you believe that!?!"

"Wow, I'm going to have to sit with this one for a while," I said. "I'm glad you were able to pass the information on. I just hope it didn't shock Mike too drastically. Messages that come out of the blue like that can rock a person's foundation. But you followed spirits' request, and now Mike knows that his younger brother is okay."

Steph's story demonstrates spirits' power to get a message across. When they reach across the veil to provide communication, they have a sense of knowing when and how everything will play out. Everything has its time, its season. So, remember—if you receive a message from a medium today that doesn't quite connect, you never know if it will tomorrow.

A Grandfather Confirmed

When I offer readings in a large, gallery-style environment, the energies are contagious. The excitement of the individuals who want to make a connection, along with the excitement of their loved ones in spirit, is high. When I come forward to communicate to a person, the experience can be nerve-racking. People are excited to receive a message, but they also find themselves a bit nervous because now everyone in the room is looking at them. Sometimes that pressure can create blocks, even when their own family member comes forward.

There was one experience in which I connected a woman to her mother, but she couldn't recognize the spirit as her mother. It wasn't until she got home and played the tape for her sister that her sister declared, "Oh, my God, that's mom!" When the woman listened to the tape again, the clarity came and the connection was made.

A similar experience occurred at one of my monthly group-reading events, when I spoke to a young woman in her thirties named Carissa.

"Hello, I'd like to bring forward a communication to you now," I said.

"Sure," Carissa responded.

"I'm aware of an older man coming forward, someone I'd place in the grandparent generation. It feels like he connects on the father's side of the family. One thing I physically feel is that he would have had a bent arm." I shifted and placed my arm in a certain position.

"Oh my God, yes, I think this may be my grandfather. It's spooky because he had a crippled arm, and he held it just like you are," Carissa said.

"Oh, very interesting. Well, he does give a few other elements. One, he shows himself with black hair, and he's looking for the food around here. Like he expected food when he arrived. He's also holding his wallet to his chest, indicating that he would have been tight with his money and responsible in giving it out. Lastly, he indicates that he wore different shoes at home than he did at work. I'm not sure if they're slippers or something else, but I see him taking his shoes off as he comes in here." I could tell that these details weren't quite connecting for Carissa. "Do these items help at all?"

"Boy, I'm not sure ... now I'm confused. The hair, the food, and the wallet reference—I don't know. And I can't recall anything about the shoes. So I'm wondering if this actually is my grandfather or someone else."

"Well, you may need to check on some of these elements. But let me bring forward his message. He tells me that you should stop worrying about what type of mother you are. You're doing great!"

Carissa wiped her eyes.

"He also tells me that you were his favorite, and that the stress you are going through right now will ease up and everything will be just fine. It may take about six months, but it will work out. So I leave you with his message and support," I concluded.

I could tell that the message connected with Carissa, but that there was a desire from her to really know who it was. About eight months passed before Carissa and I crossed paths again, and it was exciting to hear the update from her. She told me that the day after her reading, she shared the session with her father, and he was able to verify all the information that she didn't know.

"I couldn't believe it, Troy. I felt a bit silly afterward, because I said that this gentleman having black hair didn't make sense if it was Grandpa. But then my dad pointed out that Grandpa had to have some color hair before it was gray. Also, in terms of the food reference, my dad said that there was always food on the table when my grandfather came home, so it made perfect sense. Also, my grandfather didn't wear slippers but he did change shoes when he got home from work. That was something I didn't know, but my father did—actually, he didn't recall it at first but upon thinking about it he remembered. And about the money, yes, Grandpa held the purse strings and would distribute money from his wallet to my grandmother."

"Well, I'm so glad the facts became clear," I said. "It's amazing what spirit brings forward. Sometimes it doesn't make sense to us, but being able to verify it later can add another depth to the communication."

"Yes, it was a great experience and the message did make perfect sense. Also, you know how my grandpa mentioned there was something I was worried about and that it would clear up in about six months? Well, six months from our session, the thing I was worrying about did clear up. So it was great! My dad is still floored by the experience. But it was such a delight for me to see him react to the information. He was excited and emotional all at the same time. My family is so blessed to have been able to communicate with Grandpa. Thank you."

chapter

9

Meeting My Neighbor and Other Memorable Sittings

During the past ten years of studying mediumship and sharing messages from the other side, I've had some pretty remarkable experiences that still baffled me. Every time I hold a session, I ask spirit and my guides to be with me and assist me in the process. Their love and support is something I appreciate and know is there to help me. But I also know that each session provides me with a wonderful opportunity to learn something new about this work—about spirit or about the power of the soul. I'm eternally grateful, every day, for the lessons I've learned and applied to my life as a medium.

Meeting My Neighbor

People sometimes wonder whether, as a medium, I can see the future. As much as I would love to know the lottery numbers to pick or who is going to win the Super Bowl, spirit doesn't work that way with me; as a result, I'm not much of a gambler. However, the closest I've come to seeing the future came when my wife and I decided to buy a new house. We'd been living in a nine-hundred-square-foot condo for over a year, and with the birth of our son and his shift from crawling to walking, we knew we wanted something with a bit more space.

We'd been searching for a few weeks at various properties when I noticed that another condo had gone on the market. We weren't originally looking for a condo again because we wanted a home with a yard, but the minute I saw the picture on the website I did a double take. It dawned on me that I'd actually had a dream, about a year earlier, in which Chanda and I lived in one of those units. When I told Chanda about this condo she resisted at first, but when I reminded her of my dream, suddenly she wanted to know how soon we could see the property.

When we arrived at the condo, there was something very comfortable about the place. It was a three-level unit located next to a park and across the street from the school I had attended as a child. A tour through the home and the discovery that the basement bathroom had a huge Jacuzzi helped seal the deal for my wife. That same evening, we put in an offer.

When we moved in, we discovered that one of our neighbors had recently passed away. Her unit was unoccupied until the family decided what to do with her belongings. Our family would often joke with us and ask whether Chanda and I had met our neighbor. We'd learned that her passing had actually occurred at the hospital, so we didn't figure her spirit would be lingering around her home. However, if we did sense something "off" in our home, we'd often jokingly say, "Okay, neighbor, you can go back to your unit now."

Time passed, and about a year after moving in, I received a phone call from a woman who was interested in having a session with me. I didn't think much of it because I had been holding a number of sessions in our home lately. I scheduled the appointment and gave the woman my address. A few weeks later the doorbell rang.

"Hello, you must be Gina?" I said as I welcomed her in.

"Yes, thanks," Gina responded.

As we made our way into the living room and as Gina sat down on my couch, I became aware of an older woman's spirit standing about halfway up my stairs to the second floor. I acknowledged her presence, thinking that it was a bit strange to see someone coming down from that area of my home. As I began the communication, I shared messages from a few different spirits, and then I became aware again of the older woman on the staircase.

> "Okay, Gina. Now I'm aware of an older woman who is actually walking down the stairs of my home here. She's actually very comfortable in this space and feels like she owns the joint," I said. "She's a motherly figure who would have been particular on how she wanted things done. But I feel that when it came to her own home, she may have let a few things slide. She's a bit of a thinner woman, and I feel as though she would have had a disease that took her life. Does this sound like someone that you would recognize?"
>
> Gina responded with a big smile. "Yes."

I continued on with the communication, and there were also a few more spirits that came to visit her. I concluded the session as I normally do, with a brief meditation, and when we were finished, I asked Gina if she had any questions. What came out of her mouth next was not what I was expecting.

"Troy, I have to tell you something that I don't think you're going to believe. In fact, my heart is racing on how crazy this is," she said.

"Okay, what is it?"

"When we set up the appointment last week and you gave me your address, I didn't think twice about it. I just wrote it down. Then, as I began driving here, I realized that this route seemed very familiar. When I pulled into your driveway, I almost had a heart attack," she said.

"Okay, what, what is it!?!" I was very perplexed.

"You know the motherly spirit that felt very comfortable walking around your home?" she asked.

"Yes."

"Well, she's not my mother, she's my step-mom. Actually, she's not technically my step-mom but she dated my dad long enough to be … anyway, what I'm trying to tell you, Troy, is that she lived right next to you," Gina said with amazement.

"What?" I said, a bit shocked.

"Yes, the woman who knew the layout of your home so well, knew it because her unit is identical to yours … she was your neighbor!" Gina declared.

"Oh, my God, are you kidding me?"

"No, I can't believe it myself. When I drove up to your unit and realized that you lived right next to my step-mom, and then to have her come forward and give the communication the way she did, it was amazing. I didn't want to say anything before we began … "

"I'm glad you didn't," I told her. "I can't believe it. Here I've been living in this condo for over a year, and I finally got to meet my neighbor! Wow, this is a bit surreal."

Both Gina and I sat there for a moment, dumbfounded. When she left I still couldn't believe what had happened. The coincidence on that one was just too crazy.

Once I had grounded myself a bit, I met up with Chanda and my son Jake at our condo's annual picnic. The condo board was discussing some plans for the upcoming year, so I didn't have time to chat with Chanda before she had to get up and return to the house to get some work done. I stayed at the meeting with Jake and looked forward to chatting with her about the experience when I got home.

About an hour later, I returned, but before I was able to share what had occurred, Chanda said, "Boy, when I got home tonight, I still felt some energy around the place. I didn't know if it was left over from the session or if our neighbor was here—anyway, I told her to go back over to her unit, and it seemed to clear things up."

I burst out laughing and then proceeded to tell Chanda that she was right on both counts: it was energy from my last session *and* it was our neighbor. We both found ourselves at a loss for words after that. One thing's for certain, though—your neighbor may not be physically present, but that doesn't mean you won't meet them at some point.

When the Cat Came

I'm often asked if I receive spirit communication from animals. Although it is not a type of communication that comes forward often in my sessions, there have been times when an animal does come forward. I share with people that all animals have a spirit and, just like humans, when an animal's physical body dies, their spirit body lives on. For some people, the bond with their pets can be stronger than their bond with other human beings, so it really is no surprise that an animal's spirit would come forward to communicate with a person. Whether it's dogs, cats, or fish, spirit is spirit, love is love, and connections are made between two worlds.

When I hold small-group events in homes, I can have anywhere from three to twelve people gathered there. I try to connect with at least one spirit for each person. It was during one such session that I learned that a spirit might also mean a pet. I had been invited over to a home to provide communication to a group of eight. As the two-hour session was drawing to a close, I connected with the last two people in the room. I had been sharing messages from a variety of loved ones in spirit, but I sensed that my last communication was going to be different.

"Hmm, this is interesting. I would like to come to the both of you now, but I have to be honest with you—I'm not getting the connection to an individual in spirit. I mean not a human in spirit. I'm becoming aware of a ... cat ... yes, a gray cat with bright eyes coming forward to communicate with you today. Boy, this is one powerful cat. I'm aware that he keeps circling you; he isn't going to let any humans through, so to speak. His energy is the strong one today, and it's just going to be him. Can you accept a gray cat in spirit?" I asked.

"Oh my God, yes," Kim said with a laugh.

"Okay, good. Now, I have to warn you I don't usually speak cat, so it's not like I'm going to go 'meow, meow, meow,'" I joked.

The group laughed, and I continued. "The kitty tells me that he was in control of the house and that he just wants you to know he's still around. Also, he references two new cats in your home but says that he can't be replaced. Does this make sense?

"Oh, yes, we just recently adopted two new cats. Oh my goodness, he could see that," she said with a bit of nervous laughter.

"Yes, and although it's good that you have more companions, your kitty wants to let you know that he'll never be replaced. Also, some people hope that I get names, but I'm not getting anything from your kitty," I said.

"That's okay, because his name is Kitty," Kim said with a smile.

"You mean your kitty's name is Kitty?"

"Yes, real original, huh?" she said. "This is so silly—I don't know why I'm crying."

"It's okay—the bond with a pet can be very strong. And in this instance, it's clear that your kitty wants to make sure you know he's okay," I said.

"Well, I'm glad," Kim said. "Although I would have liked to have heard from some people, I'm grateful to have received a message from a cat I loved so dearly!"

A Historic Connection

I love old homes. The history and energy that have passed through the walls of an old house are incredible. From the land that a home was built on, to the people who plotted the land, to all the tenants who have ever lived there, the energy and the history of a home can linger. Sometimes the spirits of yesteryears also wish to leave a message.

I've had the opportunity to hold sessions in a variety of locations. I've held sessions in modern homes, convention halls, and even on a boat. But one of the most interesting sessions occurred for me at a historic home in the Twin Cities. The minute I walked into the house I was immediately enthralled. The hardwood floors, the stained glass windows, and the sweeping great room were everything I wanted in my own home. Before I began the session, I complimented the owners on their beautiful space.

The session was a group event, so I found myself connecting with a number of people. Then I was drawn to Alex, the owner of the home. As I connected with him, I became aware of a distinguished gentleman standing behind him.

"As I come to you, Alex, I become aware of an older gentleman that connects with you. He's a very regal individual and presents himself in a three-piece suit. There is a sense that he might fall into the great-grand-father generation, but it could be farther back than that. He has a beard and pulls a timepiece or pocket watch out of his pocket, which gives me an indication that he would have been very mindful of his time. Does this sound like someone you'd recognize?" I asked.

Alex responded, "Well, I'm not sure. My grandfathers were farmers so they never would have worn fancy suits like that."

"Okay, well, let me see if I can get any other information from him. I'm aware that he connects back to the late 1800s and from what I can see ... " Suddenly, I saw my surroundings shift, and I could see this man standing on the land the house was built on. It was almost as though I had been transported back in time for a moment and saw him in connection to the land. In an instant I was back in the home in its current time.

"Wow, okay, I just had a flash of this gentleman connected to the land your house is on, or to the building of this house. I'm seeing now that he's not connected to you as a relative but connected to the house. So you may have to check on this," I told Alex.

"Okay, but there are a lot of men that probably fit that description. Can you get anything else?" Alex asked.

"Fair enough," I said. I knew that if Alex was going to take the time to research this, it would be best if he had more specific details. So I added, "He also tells me that he would not have gone by his full name, but by his initials. Something like D. T. or E. E. Manter. He would have passed with something chest-related, and this last item has some connection to me?"

I was a bit confused that this spirit made some connection to me. "Okay, I'm a bit confused here ... something in connection to me ... no, not me ... where I'm from. So there is some reference to Fargo or North Dakota or the Red River Valley, whatever this guy's industry was, there was some connection to where I'm from."

"Okay, I'll jot all this down and let you know what I find out," Alex said.

"Please do—with communication like this, it's always nice to know when it connects. But even though you may not recognize him at this moment, he does want to let you know that he's pleased with how you just recently redid a room or helped with updating something upstairs. And also that your vision for what you see next for your own property development is right on, so pursue it," I said.

"Well, for not knowing the guy, he's accurate when it comes to the message. We just recently redid one of the rooms upstairs—you wouldn't have known that— and yes, I am pursuing a new property, so it's nice to know there's support for that," Alex said with a smile.

When the session came to an end, I thanked my hosts and all who were present and went on my way. That afternoon's experience had been very interesting, and I looked forward to hearing what

Alex discovered. About a month or so later, I received an email from Alex that said the following:

Dear Troy,

I just wanted to follow up on the communication you gave to me a few months back. You asked that I do a little research on the older gentleman that came forward. Well, here is what I found.

1) You said his name was D. T. or E. E. Manter—it was actually E. P. Cantor.

2) He didn't actually build the home, but he did plat the land.

3) You said he died of something chest-related, and it was congestive heart failure.

4) You also referenced that he had some connection to you or where you are from. Well, it turns out his son, E. P. Cantor, Jr., lived in Fargo, and the family owned the Red River Mill, which is a connection to the Red River Valley.

So there you have it. I'm still not sure why he would have come forward for me, but his message was appreciated. Also, one other coincidence... we just bought a new condo down by the waterfront, on 2nd Street. After closing on the place, I learned that one of Cantor's mills was built down by the waterfront, and he once lived in a home on 2nd Street... literally just down the street from us. I guess either I'm following him or he's following me.

Thanks again,
Alex

It was reassuring to hear that the information connected for Alex. The communication taught me that although we may not be related to the spirits that come forward, we can connect with them in other ways.

Sitting with Macy

In my years as a medium, I've had the opportunity to share messages in a variety of different ways. I've done private readings, phone readings, radio readings, and large-group events at expos. At one expo, I did readings for a group of thirty to forty people. As the session was drawing to an end, I was drawn to a young girl named Macy and her mother, Tammy. I had noticed the two when they came in, as Macy was in a wheelchair and her mother had parked the wheelchair next to her seat on the aisle. I immediately could see vibrant color coming off Macy's aura, and I knew that she was a very highly evolved soul.

My experience has taught me that souls who choose to live this life with a physical disability are advanced souls who know they will experience profound spiritual growth through their physical limitations. But they are also teachers for their family, friends, and the community of people who cross their paths. At this session, I knew that Macy was going to become my teacher.

"I'd like to come now to the mother and daughter there by the aisle," I said.

Tammy looked a bit surprised and yet excited when I called to her and her daughter. Macy had severe cerebral palsy and had been confined to a wheelchair since she was an infant. She was only able to communicate through moans, and earlier during the event I had heard her moaning off and on. But when I came to her and her mother, her energy calmed and she sat there very attentively.

"As I come forward to share with you, I see a grandmother figure, who I believe is on the paternal side, wanting to connect with your daughter. She is a taller woman, very attractive and well put together— meaning she'd dress well for this occasion. Also, she was pretty 'pissed' to leave this Earth so early and wanted to have more time here. Does this sound like someone that you can recognize?"

"Yes," Tammy responded. "That would be Macy's grandmother, her dad's mom. And yeah, she dressed just like you said and would not have wanted to leave as soon as she did."

I continued. "Macy's grandma wants you to know that she watches over Macy when she's with her dad. Grandma or "mom" will also be a guide for her son when he needs it. Grandma admits she was uneasy about Macy's disability when she was alive and wishes she could have understood it better. She also wants to tell you that you are a good mother and from where she is now, she sees how much energy you give to Macy."

With tears of joy, Tammy responded, "Oh, thank you. It's comforting to know she's guiding Macy's dad. Also it's reassuring to know that she thinks I'm a good mom. I never was quite sure when she was alive."

"As Grandma connects with Macy," I said, "she acknowledges that Macy is a teacher and is at a higher level than most. Now, what's unique here is that Grandma is stepping back now and it's almost as though I'm tapping into Macy's aura ... like I'm seeing her soul just as magnificent and as beautiful as it truly is." I was holding back my own tears.

At public events, I try to disconnect from the emotional energy of the communications that come through. I simply try to be the vessel and not let my own feelings come into play, but in this instance the beauty and the power of Macy's soul caught me off-guard. I found myself so moved to be in her presence.

"You'll forgive me as I try to regain my composure. I don't usually allow my emotions to flow during readings, but Macy's energy is so intense I can't help but be moved by her beauty," I told the audience.

"Macy shares with me that she chose to come into this world the way she did so that her message can get across clearly. She is a powerful soul who sees angels and spirit guides all the time, and they are constantly around her. Also, she can travel outside of her body, where she is able to fully see her potential and purpose in this life. Macy shows me her pure essence, and it's more beautiful than you can ever imagine. Always know that Macy chose this path and she also chose you, Tammy, because she knew you'd be the perfect partner for this adventure. Her love, gratitude, and joy go with you today, that you may know all is perfect in the world," I said.

As I concluded the message Macy let out this delightful sigh. It was almost as if she wanted to put the period on the end of the sentence. As I looked around the room, I don't believe there was a dry eye in the house. Everyone could feel the power and the magnitude of Macy's soul, and her impact on the room that day will be felt for years.

Like many individuals who choose to experience this lifetime with a handicap of some sort, Macy was a truly advanced soul. The next time you see a person with a disability, don't look on them with pity or sadness. Look on them with honor, and acknowledge that this soul has come to our earthly experience to teach the world so many magnificent things.

chapter

10

A Long Time Coming

There are some people who cross your path and change your life forever. Sometimes you are immediately aware of their impact, and other times it may take a while before your connection is revealed. When I first met Peg and her partner Sheri, I never thought they'd be more than just two people I sat with at a group reading. Peg and Sheri had been partners for over twenty-five years.

Peg was a say-it-like-it-is sort of person. She wasn't afraid to be a bitch when she needed to be, but she had a laugh that was utterly contagious. She was also an incredibly wise woman who had over thirty years of experience as an astrologer. Astrology was something I knew very little about at the time I met them, but would soon learn more about as our friendship grew. Even before I started sharing messages from spirit at our first meeting Peg needed to ask me, "What's your birthday?"

It was a Saturday afternoon in early January of 2003. Peg and Sheri had come to a group event at the house of one of their friends. I had been invited because the host had seen my work at a public event. When I began the session, the first person I was drawn to was Peg.

"Well, I'm very much aware of a variety of people who are gathering all around you here. And I'd like to start with you if I may," I said, pointing at Peg.

She nodded yes, and I continued. "I'm aware of a woman standing next to you—there is a kinship or a peer-to-peer connection with you. I don't get a family link, but she would have been someone like family. Also, she is showing herself more connected to your age now, although I have a feeling she was younger than you are now when she died. This person is a real character, a great lady to hang around with, and she thinks this experience is going to be a real trip."

Peg looked inquisitively at me but did not respond yet to anything.

"She is a little bit rounder in her midsection, with short, sandy-colored, wispy hair," I said. "She's wearing a suit coat and slacks, and there's this energy that reaches out to you ... there is a sense that she would be open to this, but some reservation about who she'd do this for. She says she'd come forward for you but not for her family. Does this sound like someone you'd recognize?"

"Yes," Peg said, very stoic.

"Her message for you is ... wait, you know, it's funny. In my head, I'm thinking 'Boy, I'm glad this connects,' and this spirit is saying, 'Man, I should have made this kid work more.'"

With that line, Peg laughed and added, "You're talking to my friend Betty. You described her perfectly, from the hair down to her style of clothing. She was quite the character, and yes, she'd be more comfortable sharing a message with me than with her family."

"Well, I'm glad that she connects with you. She seems to be on a roll now, pulling out what looks like a little notebook, and she says 'Oh, oh, it's my turn to talk now ... '"

Before I could finish my sentence, Peg chimed in. "Well, it's about damn time, Betty. I've been waiting thirty years. We had a death pact: an agreement that whoever died first would come back and give the other one a message. I just didn't think it would take this frickin' long!"

We both chuckled, and then I said, "Well, she comes forward now with support and encouragement for you, and says that the path you are taking has been solid and firm and that your way of getting there is like an old pickup truck. People sometimes look at you and think *she'll never make it there with that*, and yet time and again you prove people wrong because the pickup will never break down. She also wants to make sure you share this communication with another person. Almost as though this is not just for you but for another as well. Does that make sense?" I asked.

"Yes, there were actually three of us in this death pact, including our other friend, Ester. I'll make sure to pass this message on to Ester. She'll love it," Peg told me.

"Lastly," I said, "she stops and takes a wad of keys out of her back pocket and hands you these keys ... so I don't know if she kept a lot of keys or what, but this is what she gives to you."

Peg laughed at this and added, "I believe what she's actually referencing is money. See, we used to always say that whether we thought it was right or not, money was the one thing in this physical experience that gave you the keys to the kingdom. So we'd say that if there was any way we can manifest money for the other in spirit, we'd do it, because that would actually help us here on Earth. I see now it's more important to have the keys first, then the money. Damn. I guess I can always fall back on trying to strike it rich at the casino."

The group shared a collective laugh, and it became an experience and a session that connected Peg and me. A few months after that group event, Peg and Sheri wanted to experience the connection to spirit in their own home. They invited me to their place for a private session. During that session, Sheri received a special communication from someone she loved.

"Okay, Sheri. I'm aware of a woman who would like to connect with you. I feel as though she is your mother. Your mother is in spirit, yes?"

"She is," Sheri confirmed.

"Well, as your mother stands there, she wants to give you a few more pieces of information so you know it's really her. Immediately, as I say this, I feel a 'popping' in my head and a pain here in my temple. It almost feels like something happened internally here," I said, pointing to my temple.

"Oh yes," Sheri said. "My mother died of a brain aneurism, so that pain would make sense."

I nodded in recognition and then noticed an image on Peg and Sheri's coffee table, which Sheri's mom had directed me to.

"What does this lion symbolize?" I asked. "Is that the sign for Leo?"

"Yes, why?" Sheri asked.

"Well, your mother keeps telling me that she was a Leo…"

Peg laughed out loud before I could finish. "Ha ha, leave it to your mother to reference an astrology symbol. Yes, she was in fact a Leo."

"Okay, well, since I'm clueless about astrology, I'm glad it made sense to you," I said.

I continued the communication. "Her message for you is to let you know she wants to make amends for not being there for you in the mornings when you were younger. She keeps showing me this image of you being alone in the mornings. Does this make sense?"

"Yes," Sheri said with emotion. "My mother was a waitress and worked nights when I was growing up. So in the mornings I always had to get myself up, get ready for school, and make my own breakfast because my mom was always sleeping. So yes, her message makes perfect sense. Thanks, Mom."

• • •

My friendship with Peg and Sheri continued to grow over the next few years. Chanda and I would occasionally have them over for dinner or vice versa. We'd exchange services: I'd offer them mediumistic readings, and they would give Chanda and me insight into our astrological charts. We even found out how truly small a world it was: Peg was from Burlington, North Dakota (Chanda's hometown), Chanda had graduated from high school with Peg's nephew, and Peg's brother had done some remodeling for Chanda's parents. So it many respects, it was almost like all of our souls were destined to connect. Chanda would also go on to study tarot and astrology under Peg and Sheri.

Peg and Sheri's insight into our astrological chart was something both Chanda and I enjoyed. Even though I wasn't quite sure whether I believed everything was laid out in the planets, it was fun to learn about what might be possible on my journey. And Peg informed me once that it makes sense, astrologically speaking, for me to be a medium in this lifetime. A Neptune Sun conjunction in Sagittarius, with the Moon in the twelfth house, means that I have the tendency to either do work as a medium or be a drunk—the choice was mine, and they were glad to see I'd gone with the mediumship option.

We also learned that Chanda and I made a good pair, and that in August of 2005 something significant was going to happen. Having this astrological glimpse of the future was exciting, in that it provided a sense of peace to know that we'd only have to "hold out" for two more years, until that August, and then all would be well. But not exactly knowing what "something significant" meant also left us with a few questions.

When you're floating in a close connection with friends, you always assume that it's going to stay that way. So when we discovered, several years later, that Peg had come down with cancer, we were shocked. Peg recovered from the initial bout and was able to go home from the hospital. However, she was back and forth having test after test, and ultimately it was revealed that she had cancer in her lungs and bronchial tubes, and it was spreading throughout her whole body.

My first visit with Peg and Sheri after Peg's cancer diagnosis was on August 8, 2005. What prompted our meeting was a dream I'd had, the night before, about the two of them. When I arrived at their home, I shared the details:

In my dream, the two of you called me and asked me to visit. When I arrived, Peg, you were in bed and you were very uncomfortable, having hot flashes and sweating. Collectively, spirit came forward to let you know they were holding or catching you in this protective net—it looked like a silver or crystal hammock. As I shared the message, Peg, you became uncomfortable in the bed because you didn't like the idea of being kept alive. Sometimes the pain was too great, and you didn't like the idea that something was keeping you alive.

Spirit shared that the net wasn't there to protect or to heal; there was no sense of obligation to heal or shift or transform if you didn't want to. The net was simply there to be a safe haven for whatever choice you made. There were other friends and family in the dream that wanted you to heal. You didn't like the idea of someone thrusting their desires on you.

Then a shorter man in spirit came forward who had been in the Navy—maybe a family link, on the father's side of the family. He came forward just to offer support and to let his presence be known. After the gentleman finished his communication, we gathered on the beach and all of us held hands in a circle. There was this mantra about being connected to the universe. As we repeated it, we could feel this pulsing pass into our hands, through our chests, and then down our other arm and out our hand into the next person's hand. There was a collective experience of being completely connected, as one and as spirit. After that experience, I went home, and the next night I received a call around 4:40 or 4:42 in the morning to come and support you on your transition to the other side. But before I could make it to your house, I woke up.

Peg and Sheri listened to me with curiosity as I shared my dream. When they'd digested the information, Sheri said, "Well, first off, the spirit that came forward has to be my father."

Peg added, "That's right. I was thinking the same thing with the Navy connection."

"My dad died when I was only three, but he had just gotten out of the Navy, and, from what I know about him, he would have been a shorter man. Wow, it's comforting to know he's with you now," Sheri said to Peg.

"It's also interesting that the time 4:40 to 4:42 came up, since that was the time of death for my mother," Peg said. "There's a lot to digest here … but it's significant because we've just been discussing various options, such as bringing in hospice and speeding up the process just a tad. I just love this idea of a silver hammock, because that's the feeling I've had over the past few days. So thank you, Troy, for sharing your dream. It's comforting to know that spirit is here."

As we wrapped up our evening, we made plans to meet every Monday night to connect with spirit. Peg saw this as an opportunity to build her connection as she entered the last phase of her life, and I saw it as a moment to support and be with a friend during this very intimate personal transition. In many respects, I saw Peg as my own Morrie Schwartz. I knew that she would be educating me through this process, and I joked with her that if Mitch Albom had *Tuesdays with Morrie,* then I would have PMs with Peg.

As we meet throughout the month of August, we all found it interesting that two years earlier we had discussed August 2005 as being significant for me—little did we know that it would be in this way. We joked about how we had assumed that "something significant" would be something like a job change or a move. It turned out that the significant moment was being with a dying friend. Definitely not what any of us had ever expected.

Our sessions continued through September and October, and, with each passing week, our bond grew and Peg's body continued to give way. When you know a friend is dying, you try to prepare yourself for the loss, but you never know if the last time you see them is the *last* time you'll see them. The last time I saw Peg alive was October 24, 2005. We had our traditional Monday night gathering, connecting with spirit and watching a DVD we'd come to love. It was called *Star Gaze*, and it was images of the Hubble Space Telescope set to New Age music. Peg, Sheri, and I all loved it because we imagined that it is what Peg would get to experience when she crossed over. As I left that evening, I didn't think it would be the last time I'd see her.

In fact, another week went by; on Monday night, October 31, 2005, I'd planned to hold my evening with Peg and Sheri but then decided to reschedule since my in-laws were in town and it was Halloween, so I'd be taking my son around trick-or-treating. Chanda, Jake, and I were visiting at my mother's house when I received a phone call on my cell phone—from Sheri. When I heard her voice, I immediately knew something was wrong. She told me that Peg had passed.

I shared the news with Chanda and my family, and they were all very supportive. I left our Halloween Party and drove to Peg and Sheri's house. On my way, various thoughts flashed through my mind. Why hadn't I gone there that night? Why didn't I sense that it was happening? If I had a link to spirit, why wouldn't I have felt it the moment it happened?

When I arrived at the house, Peg's body was lying on the bed. I embraced Sheri and then sat down next to Peg and took her hand. This was the first time I'd ever been with a body that had just died. Of course, I'd been to a number of funerals where people were embalmed, but this experience was very different. I was only by Peg's side for a few moments when it became so very clear to me that she was not there. Her spirit, her essence, had definitely moved on—it didn't make sense for me to be sitting and holding her hand. So I moved over and sat by Sheri to comfort her. The whole experience was very surreal. We didn't exchange many words, and there was a sacred silence. We knew Peg was on a great adventure, returning to the source and seeing her family.

A few days later, Peg was cremated and Sheri had a memorial service. Peg didn't want anything fancy, let alone a traditional church service, so all of her friends and family piled into a smaller side room at the funeral home, standing room only, and we shared stories and songs from Peg's life.

As part of the service, I played scenes from the *Star Gaze* DVD that Peg had loved so much. As the awe-inspiring images from the Hubble Space Telescope played on the projector, I shared with people that these were the things Peg was now seeing on her journey, and that her greatest joy was knowing that she could be among the stars and planets she'd been studying for so many years.

In many ways, it was perfect that Peg had died on Halloween. Sheri often said she'd wanted to go out on a memorable date, and since Halloween is said to be the night of spirits, it seemed fitting that Peg would choose that night to join the spirit world.

As the weeks went by following Peg's death, I continued to meet with Sheri once a month. The gatherings were not only to check in on Sheri's well-being, but to also help her make that connection to Peg in spirit. Of course, we both hoped Peg would make her spirit known to us immediately. Others had been having dreams about her, but Sheri and I were still waiting to make the connection. Peg had been the first person I knew, who had died, who had fully known what I did as a medium, and she was one of the people who supported me the most. So both Sheri and I had thought that Peg's communication would come quick and strong. However, since Peg and I had been so close, I knew it would be hard for me to trust my own impressions. As a medium, I rarely tried to connect with the spirits of my own friends or family members since it was hard for me to discern the communication.

When Sheri and I first got together, we declared to Peg's spirit that we wanted some form of physical communication from her. Peg had always collected bells, so we determined that Peg would be giving us a sign when we heard three bells. So from that moment forward, we were waiting for bells. In fact, we'd even set some of Peg's bells out during our sessions to see if she would ring them. What we learned is that staring at a bell doesn't make it ring. We had to have faith that when the moment was right, we'd hear the bells and know that Peg was near.

As a medium, I receive communication from spirit in very subtle ways. It's a very rare occasion that it blares right into my face, but with Peg I thought it would be different. It wasn't until about a month after her passing that I realized her communication would come in just the same way it does with other spirits—in very subtle ways.

One evening, I was conducting one of my group sessions. We were holding the event at Peg and Sheri's beading shop, and it was the first night that I sensed Peg clearly. She didn't come forward to communicate to anyone; I just had the sense of her being there. It was almost as if she was looking on from the back of the room and saying, "This is cool—I get to see how these evenings work from the other side now." This connection was comforting, but I still wanted something clear … I still wanted those bells.

As the months passed, Sheri and I continued to meet. A business trip took me to Washington, DC, and little did I think it would be in our nation's capitol where I would receive the communication I had been longing for ever since Peg's passing.

My trip to Washington was reminiscent of my trip there a year earlier. Being in television production, I always attended an annual conference where producers and networks converged to hear and pitch new TV program ideas. After a day full of seminars and presentations, plus an evening dinner, I had returned to my hotel room to get a good night's sleep before the next day of seminars. It was in my dream state that the communication with Peg began.

I was at a home. Everything appeared normal, and I was sitting on my couch when I heard the phone.

Ring, Ring, Ring

I went to grab the phone, and said, "Hello."

What I heard on the other end was not what I expected. "Hi, Troy, it's Peg!"

A bit confused, I asked, "Who?"

Peg said again, "It's Peg. Sheri and I are going to talk to you on Wednesday through my niece."

I couldn't believe what I was hearing. This was Peg's voice, alive and well. I had to sit down on the couch because I couldn't catch my breath, and I began hyperventilating.

Peg said, "Troy, it's okay, it's me."

I yelled down the hall, "Chanda, come here, come here."

Chanda ran to me in the living room, saying, "What, what is it!?!"

"Here, take the phone and say hello. Say hello," I said excitedly.

"Hello? Hello?" Chanda said. "There's no one there."

I grabbed the phone. "Hello! Hello!"

There was nothing but silence on the line. With my heart racing, I was about to explain that Peg was on the phone when..."

RING, RING, RING.

A fire alarm woke me. It blared three times in a row.

RING, RING, RING.

My room was dark, and I jolted around trying to get my bearings. I glanced at the clock and saw that it was 5:30 in the morning. In my head I was thinking, "Peg, is this your way of ringing the bell? Is there really a fire, or did this dream make me hear this alarm?"

Then the fire alarm stopped. I looked out my door and out the window to see if anyone else was reacting to what I'd heard. The halls were quiet. I stumbled back into my hotel room and immediately sat down at my computer to email Sheri and Chanda. Peg's voice in my dream had been so vivid: "Troy, it's

Peg!" Then to be woken by the sound of three bells—it was a one/two punch that I knew was more than just a coincidence.

The impact of that dream communication was profound. I felt an intense sense of peace knowing that Peg was okay and that she was reaching out to connect with me. For years I'd been telling people to trust their dreams because they're a powerful way to receive communication. Now here I was, having one of those powerful dreams myself.

Peg's communication has continued to come, in various ways, in the years since her passing. She's even come forward for communication to some of her friends through my work as a medium. It's always a unique experience to sit with someone and then suddenly see Peg standing in the background. But she knows how I work, and she's good at bringing forward information that I wouldn't know about her or about the person I'm sitting with. Peg has also become a guiding force for Sheri, Chanda, and me. In many respects, her passing has increased the bond between the three of us. We became like the Three Musketeers, and Peg's spirit became a motivator for us to take leaps in our lives that we never would have if not for Peg's influence. She is a dear friend, and a spirit I'm glad to have in my corner.

PART THREE

What's It All Mean?

chapter

11

Taking the Leap

We all face moments in life that push us beyond our comfort zone. We experience a turning point where the path we've been on changes and the person we once were evolves into someone else. These moments at the edge are where we discover who we really are, and what we are truly capable of.

The big leap occurred for me on May 2, 2007. Chanda and Jake and I were about to embark on a six-week journey—and the beginning of my life as a full-time medium. I'd just left my job of seven years as a television producer/director, and I'd been featured on the local NBC station's ten o'clock news about my mediumship work. As a family, we planned to fly from Minneapolis to Portland and then drive down the Pacific Coast to Los Angeles. There we would catch a flight to Hawaii, where we'd be staying for two weeks before traveling to Montana for two weeks of sessions.

This leap wasn't something that happened overnight. Most leaps aren't that immediate. My shift from the full-time job to focus fully on my work as a medium had been incubating ever since my first astrology reading with Peg. But the excitement and the uncertainty of this new leap was something you can never prepare for. With each step, you also hope that there are "signs" from above to help you know you are on the right track.

For Chanda and me, the signs we needed came right away. As I pulled into the driveway after finishing my last day of work as a TV producer and was greeted by Chanda and Jake, we heard these lyrics over the radio: "What kind of world do you want? Think anything."

The lyrics came from the hit song "World" by the band Five for Fighting. The power of this song's message reassured Chanda and me that we were in fact creating our new world together, even if just through our thoughts. As the song continued, it was like the words were meant just for us and our new journey. We'd of course heard the expression "be careful what you wish for" many times, and we realized that this new beginning was exactly what we had been wishing for. We also understood that our new history was starting... NOW.

On our six-week trip we experienced many beautiful new things, and we began to understand the ups and downs of producing events in new locations. At the heart of it, the most profound signs that we were on the right path came from the messages we received from spirit with the people we met in readings. However, one of the most inspiring messages from spirit came from an unlikely source.

My Father... the Medium?

Before we flew from Minneapolis to Portland, we made a stop at my father's home in a suburb outside of Minneapolis. My dad was very excited about our new endeavor, yet nervous at the same time. Although he had encouraged me to expand my wings and explore other options beyond the company I worked for, I don't think he was quite ready to have me say that I was leaving my job to pursue mediumship work. Throughout my journey as a medium, my dad had been a huge support. He would always acknowledge that he didn't quite understand nor always agree with my perspectives, but he was always there to listen.

As we were discussing our plans with my dad and his girl-friend, Mary, he handed me a card.

"Here, son, this is for you."

"And read it out loud," Mary said.

"Well, thank you." I opened the card.

What I read next I wasn't quite prepared for.

I first read the front of the card: *"Wheresoever you go, go with all your heart. —Confucius."*

I continued to the inside of the card:

"Memo: Inspired by Grandpa Leonard and delivered by his Son.

No spirit is more vulnerable yet more resilient than the Human Spirit. It transcends time in ways that most cannot understand and dare not consider, let alone believe. Yet it exists, a gift of the Universe to those who open themselves to explore its reality. You have a key to unlock these doors—to help the broken, distraught, and lonely realize there is much to be shared from the vastness of this universe. We who have passed over often reach out, but too often cannot touch.

You, Troy, lift us, and lift those who dare to explore the continuum of the Spirit, ultimately connecting us in ways that truly matter. Your integrity, honesty, and sensitivity light a path that is comforting to the many who wonder if it might be true. Serve many with this gift, and you will be richly blessed in ways you have not yet conceived. Continue to nourish that resilient Spirit that exists in us all. Through inspirational words, thoughts, and actions, you will be God's blessing to many. Be humble, and those needing your insights shall appear as often as you attract them.

Just so you know, I brag about you up here and give out lots of refer-rals. Your dad probably doesn't really know how much he was inspired to write the above but trust me, he was. And even though I used to stick my tongue out at you, ask about your girlfriends, and be silly with you, I thought it important that you carry these thoughts in your heart as you write this new chapter in your life.

I always told your dad to carry some emergency money tucked away in his wallet, and to this day he does. I also told him to make sure you had some there too. Grandma says to travel safely, and she and I send our love and light...

P.S. Grandpa Ed is giving you two thumbs-up!

As I read the card aloud, I got choked up. I was incredibly touched to receive such encouragement before we left on our journey. I was very proud of my dad for trusting his own abilities and allow-ing this inspiration from his father to come through. I couldn't help but reflect on how instrumental my Grandpa Leonard had been in my mediumship development. It was reassuring to know he was still rooting for us—and that my mother's father, Grandpa Ed, was too.

Hello, McFly!

Our journey out west was an exciting one, and it was the first time I'd ever been to the Pacific Northwest. Portland was beauti-ful, and it was exciting for me to visit the city where *What the Bleep Do We Know!?*, a wonderful film about quantum physics and the power of thought, was set. Chanda and I gave readings at a small new age bookstore called *Healing Waters, Sacred Spaces*. It was the type of shop I could spend hours in, with great books on metaphysics, beautiful crystals and stones, and an assortment of small eclectic practitioner rooms.

During my last session at the bookstore, I met a man named Steve and his wife, Janet. When you work at a bookstore in a city you are not from, the host will generally schedule the sessions for you. For this particular session, all I knew was that I'd be sitting with a man named Steve and that he had paid in cash. The significance of that would be revealed later.

When Steve and his wife arrived, I introduced myself and welcomed them. I could sense Steve's nervous energy and noticed that he had brought a digital recorder to the session.

"Do you mind if I record this?" Steve asked.

Since I taped each session myself, I replied, "No, not at all. I believe it's always important for people to tape their sessions, so having two recordings will guarantee that we get something on the tape."

Steve and his wife smiled, knowing that they would have a backup.

I began the session as I normally do, with an overview of how I work and the simple request that after I describe who comes forward, all I need is a simple "yes" or "no" response from the person as to whether or not they recognize the spirit. This ensures that the people I sit with don't give me any additional information.

As the session began, I became aware of a young spirit coming forward, and I began to share what I saw.

> "I'm aware of a young girl in spirit who would like to come forward," I said. "She's blond, in her teens, and she says she's family. She also tells me she died very quickly with an impact." I slapped my hands to represent the sensation I was feeling.
>
> I could tell that Steve was beginning to recognize the person coming forward.
>
> "I also feel as though her passing was some time ago. She gives me a very hot or warm feeling around her neck, which is an indication that she could have had some pain or injury there. She says that she saw this as an opportunity to sneak in, as a springboard to communicate. Yes or no—would you be able to recognize this person?"

Steve spoke up at once. "Yes, I believe that's my cousin. She died in a car accident thirty-two years ago with a broken neck. She was blond, just like you described her."

"Well, she wants you to know she's here, and she's wanting you to pass the message on to the rest of her family, that she is all right and that she is with them," I concluded.

Steve sat in amazement as he received this communication from his cousin. He hadn't thought of her in years, and here she was, dropping by to say hello after all this time. But then I brought forward another spirit.

"I'm aware now of a gentleman, a young man in spirit. This young man is coming forward but he says, 'ladies first.' I'm aware of a family link, and as he sits here, it's as if he is back in the corner, inquisitively observing. As if he's trying to figure this out," I explained to Steve and Janet. "He's 'no GQ model.' He wouldn't have seen himself that way, but there is a confidence to him. He says he had some stomach issues; there's a pain."

Steve said, "Yes."

"As he's coming forward, I feel like I'm his friend. I just met him, but I'm aware of him including me right now. He would want to pick everyone, so no one would be last to get chosen on the team. No one gets left out. A very caring nature. As he puts it, 'I'm an old soul.' There's an old nature, wisdom, to him. Physical sensations I feel are, like, urinary tract, burning of some kind. In his mind, during the latter stages of his life, there's a heaviness that occurs, that wears on him. He wants to shout from the top of the steeple that he is free of that now. There is no more pain; he's running the race now he wishes he could have run here. He's a little proud of this; he wants you to know how fast he can go."

At this point, tears streamed down both Steve and his wife's faces. I asked if they could recognize the individual, and they said yes.

"That's our son, Christopher Buckmaster. He died of cancer, and yes, he would have been the type of person to let women go first. And you would have been his friend," Steve informed me.

With this acknowledgment, their son's communication came on more rapidly.

"The love he felt from the two of you during this, and the love he feels now, is constant. He continues to repeat over and over again, 'You will not forget me or what I look like.' How could you forget a face like that? I know it won't take away the pain, or the emptiness in your hearts, but he wants you to know this is his opportunity to say, 'I made it.' He never doubted he would make it, but he needs you to know he did. He acknowledges that your faith is strong, but you didn't sign up for this; you didn't want to go through this."

What happened next was something I wasn't prepared for, and it has never come forward in my communications since. However, it is a perfect example of how it's not up to the medium to decide what comes forward and what doesn't. Whatever I receive should just be given.

"He says, 'Hello, McFly.' He's calling you George McFly. There's this whole McFly connection," I said, perplexed.

"Oh, gosh," Steve said. "Troy, from the time our son was six or seven, he had an obsession with the *Back to the Future* trilogy. At one point our garage was transformed into Universal Studios, complete with a model of the DeLorean that kids could ride in! In his teens and early twenties, people used to call him the 'movie guy' because he always had a movie line to quote for any situation. One of his favorites, and one that he quoted to me, was the line you just quoted: 'Hello, McFly. Think McFly, think!'"

As the session continued, the bond between Chris and his parents continued, and the touching experience caused both father and mother to weep. At the end of the session, Steve shared his final thoughts, which reminded me again why our journey to Portland was truly a journey of service.

"Thank you so much for this incredible reading. I don't know where to begin to tell you how much it meant to us and how it has profoundly affected our lives. It makes perfect sense that Chris chose to come to you. He was a filmmaker as well, and during his final stages of cancer, he produced an eighteen-minute documentary film about children with cancer. Paul Newman even helped fund it. As a science teacher, I'm always looking for solid evidence. I began this search to find out if I could make contact with my son through a psychic medium. This was part of an experiment, which is why I paid cash ahead of time and registered with only my first name," Steve told me.

"I knew subjectively that my son was communicating with me," Steve added, "but I was seeking objective proof. When a stranger I've never met, from thousands of miles away, tells me things about my son or other relatives who have passed that they could not possibly know, I feel I have found that proof. Proof that consciousness survives that which we call death. I may not understand how these things happen, but they do happen."

Chris' communication to his father and mother is one message I don't think I'll ever forget. Not only was he able to bring his sense of humor forward, but he was able to blend his awareness and joy about movies with my awareness. Together, we were able to bring forward the evidence that helped his father and mother truly know it was him. As a father myself, I leave sessions like Chris' with a new appreciation for the bond between parents and children. It teaches me not to take my own connection with my son for granted. And now I always return to my son after sessions and smother him with hugs and kisses.

A Spirit Never Dies

We left Portland and set off down the coast of Oregon. Our first stop on this part of our journey was a group session for a crowd of around fifteen to twenty people. This was a special event for me because it was the first time Chanda would join me in a presentation. Chanda had been developing her work as an intuitive over the years and had always been there to support me. Now it was her turn to share her messages of inspiration as well.

Throughout the evening, Chanda and I volleyed back and forth between people giving messages. In group events, I always tend to get a sense of who I will be going to. As Chanda was finishing up one of her messages, I became aware of this young woman in spirit standing next to a woman in the front row. When Chanda completed her message to another member of the audience, I stood up and began the communication.

"I'd like to come to you if I may," I said.

"Yes, thank you," she responded.

"I'm aware of a young woman in spirit coming forward. She's in her early thirties and a pretty girl, standing tall as she comes forward. There's a very loving energy that comes from her and it's almost like she's an angel on your shoulder. Yes or no—do you have a daughter in spirit?" I asked.

The woman looked a bit shocked to hear this communication. She stumbled on her words and said, "No? ... I mean, yes ... I mean, I was pregnant at one time about thirty years ago but I had a miscarriage. I never knew the sex of the child, but I always felt it was a girl." She managed to say this before breaking down.

There was a sigh from the crowd at this intimate detail about this woman's life and journey.

"Well, she is wanting to come forward to let you know she's always been with you," I said. "She also understands why you made the choice that you did. She says you can forgive yourself now. She's okay, and her spirit, although it was only in your body for a brief time, still connects with you."

The woman, in tears, said, "Oh, thank you. It's been something that has been on my mind for over thirty years. I always sensed her near me. Please let her know that I love her."

"She knows," I said.

That moment was a very profound one for everybody in attendance. It highlighted the power of spirit and that regardless of the stage of development a fetus is in during a pregnancy, a soul does have a purpose. This communication also taught me that we are not to judge; each soul's journey happens for an intended reason, and a spirit never truly dies. Whatever the journey is for a mother and a baby, whether their soul bond is to experience a miscarriage, an abortion, or a stillbirth, those little souls have a purpose and a mission, not only for themselves but also for the lives they come in contact with.

Michael, Row Your Boat Ashore

In the United States, there are a number of cities that have become known as spiritual meccas. Places that for whatever reason have an energy and a feeling about them that draw people from all walks of life to the area—places like Sedona, Arizona, or Ashville, North Carolina. There's a town along Oregon's coastline that I'd wanted to visit for years, a little college town called Ashland. Ashland is best known for its famous Shakespeare Theatre Company, but it is also home to Neale Donald Walsch, the author of *Conversations with God*. When I was first starting my journey in Boston, the *Conversations with God* series had a profound impact on me and my concept of God.

The city of Ashland also had become the home of filmmaker Stephen Simon, who produced *Somewhere in Time* and *What Dreams May Come*. Stephen had moved to Ashland after leaving Hollywood, and partnered with his friends James Twyman and Neale Donald Walsch to create the movie *Indigo*. Stephen created a whole new movement of Spiritual Cinema. As a filmmaker, it was thrilling to know that both the spiritual world and my creative filmmaking world could coincide.

I had organized a group event at an extraordinary library in Ashland called the Rogue Valley Metaphysical Library. The session was on a Saturday afternoon, and when the time came to share my work, it was with a very intimate group of five or six people. Having done a number of sessions throughout the years, I had come to understand that the people who are meant to be there, are, and those that aren't, aren't. In every city that we visited it was clear that spirit would teach me something, and the connections would be with whoever they needed to be.

During this session in Ashland, one communication stands out. It brought me a whole new appreciation for the song "Michael, Row Your Boat Ashore."

"Hi, I'd like to come forward to you, if I may. What's your name?" I asked the woman sitting across from me.

"Sure. I'm Jessica," she said with a smile.

"Jessica, I'm aware of a woman who is wanting to come forward to you. She's a little bit shorter and rounder and from what she's showing me, she had curly hair. There's a maternal feeling to her. Does this sound like someone you'd recognize?"

"Well, it could be two different people," Jessica said.

"Okay, well, let me see what else she can give me. I feel like she would be comfortable with this type of communication and . . . "

Before I could finish my thought, lyrics to a song entered my head, loud and clear. "I don't know why, but I'm hearing music," I said, "but it's the song "Michael, Row Your Boat Ashore." Does that make sense?"

Jessica looked a little stunned, gasped, and then let out a big laugh. "Oh my, yes. I feel like the room is spinning a bit. "Michael, Row Your Boat Ashore" was my mentor Mely's favorite song. In fact, the last time I saw her as she was dying, she requested that I sing that song.

"Wow." Even I was a bit shocked that the song had connected so clearly.

"Yes," she said. "Mely—Filomena Naces—was a Filipino psychic surgeon who passed away a few years ago. I've just written a book about her, and I'm trying to decide what to do with it."

I then stood up from my chair and walked toward the bookshelves that were in the room. I continued: "Mely says, 'Oh, that Jessica. She's always talking about books. She wants to know everything that's going on with books.' Mely also says, "Oh yes, it's a book about me. No, it's going to be a movie, and I'm going to be on Oprah.'"

Jessica said, "I still can't quite believe this. I've never met you before, yet here you are singing the favorite song of a friend of mine who died several years ago. Ask her...oh boy, I feel like I should ask her another question to really clarify who she is..."

I interjected. "She tells me to say, 'What? "Michael Row Your Boat Ashore" isn't enough?'"

Jessica laughed and so did the group.

"'Well,' she says, 'I'm finished. Where's the food? Let's eat!'"

"Okay, that connects too and confirms it's her. Almost every event in the Filipino culture begins and ends with the eating of large quantities of food. Oh, thank you, Troy, and thank you, Mely, for your message."

After the session, Jessica informed me that Mely had done work as a medium when she was alive—that was why, Jessica believed, her communication had come across so clearly.

My experience in Ashland was short and sweet, but being able to share my work in a town that had inspired me was a rewarding experience. I also knew that I'd never hear the song "Michael, Row Your Boat Ashore" again without thinking of this communication.

A Message in Montana

Our journey continued down the Pacific Coast. We had group events in San Francisco, a gallery event at the famous Bodhi Tree Bookstore in West Hollywood, and two weeks in Hawaii for R&R and a holistic expo. We returned home to Fargo for forty-eight hours before hitting the road again, for two weeks in Montana. As a family, we'd never been to Montana before, so we were excited to see the beauty of the mountains and sit under the famed big sky.

Our work was to take place at a quaint little holistic bookstore in Missoula called the Feng Shui Center. I was to hold a public event there and then do some private readings. I had first been invited to a house, just outside of Missoula, to lead a small-group session.

As I drove toward the home for the group session, I was awestruck by the beauty of the mountains before me. This was truly God's country, and I could understand why the producers of *What Dreams May Come* had chosen the mountains of Montana to represent the afterlife. It brought me a sense of peace, knowing that this beauty would surround me as I shared messages that morning. When I arrived at the home, the whole family was already there and ready for the communication.

Immediately, I could sense a young man coming forward. There are times during sessions when I immediately know which spirit will be coming first, and in this instance, it was clear he had a message for everyone there.

"Thanks for having me here this morning. It's a pleasure to connect with all of you, and I want to start off with a gentleman who is wanting to come forward right away. He stands at the edge of the kitchen and in many respects I feel like he is going to connect with everyone in some way. He is a younger man and an individual who would have passed early in life. I'd maybe place him in his late teens or early twenties. He was a bigger man than I am; I'm 5'10" and he seems to stand taller than that," I said.

As I gave the communication, I could start to see the reactions in the room. It was as if everyone had been holding their breath, and as this young man's communication came forward, everyone took a collective sigh. People's eyes were darting around, and I could tell that it was connecting for the whole group.

"The first sense I got from him is that he's a bit of a joker," I told them. "He wishes he had some chains and could rattle the rafters; he wants to haunt you all in a joking way and do the whole scary factor in the way that he comes forward."

The family all chuckled at this.

"When he came forward, I felt a yawn. It's 10:30 AM now, and I feel he's saying that it's still too early for him. Like he would need to be sleeping in, or need a nap. He's also wondering where breakfast is. And he'd want to make sure he had that opportunity. Once he's confident about something, he wants to make sure he can do it on his own. So there is a showy nature that comes from him. He's very mindful of the elders. I can hear the song "You've Got the Cutest Little Baby Face," which means he'd have been known for his baby face. Out of respect, he connects with you first, Grandma. Does this sound like someone you'd recognize?" I asked.

"Yes, I think so, but say more," she responded.

I continued. "He says I better go to you first if I know what's good for me. He says, 'You're so great, you'd remember me perfectly, you know.' And so what he's here to say is that he's still riding, and 'Listen, if I was here I'd be making fun of you all.' He would be in the other room joking about it rather than being here. He also tells me that he realizes he got the shaft. He sees now that it wasn't an accident, that everything that occurred was all part of the process. He couldn't have seen that until he got where it was. Does this make sense?"

"Yes, this sounds like my grandson Clint. He died unexpectedly just a few months ago," she said.

"Now he wants to connect with Mom. I'm being drawn over to you here on the floor. Are you Mom?" I asked the woman.

"Yes, I'm the mom, I'm Nikki," she said, wiping her eyes.

"I have to chuckle a bit as he tries to sit on the floor next to you. He is a bit awkward and clumsy as he gets down on the floor. He tells me you were free with the language or had a sharp tongue. He says he knows you think this is shitty. Nothing that he will say here will take away the sadness or the loss that exists. What he does want to say, or, I should say, sing, is the song "On Eagles' Wings." He's not a great singer, and he admits it's a little cheesy, but he wants you to know that he is up there on eagles' wings," I concluded.

With that piece of information, Nikki cried more and through her tears said, "Yeah, I guess you could say I think his death is shitty. But his message about eagles' wings is perfect." She reached into her pocket and pulled out a laminated clipping that had a picture of Clint on one side and the lyrics to "On Eagles' Wings" on the other.

She then said, "It was the song we had at his funeral, and I had these made as a little memorial for him. Thank you so much for bringing his message forward. It's been so hard for our family to have him die so young. Connecting with you at least gives us a little reassurance that he's okay."

Nikki and her family were still healing from the loss of her son. Clint had been a healthy eighteen-year-old kid, and then one day he was running in a field and his heart just stopped. It was a huge help in the family's grieving process to know that Client was truly okay.

During our six-week journey we covered a lot of ground. We flew over 8,200 miles and drove over 3,000 miles—that's over 11,200 miles total, or the equivalent of traveling from Los Angeles to New York five times. It was an opportunity to learn to trust spirit's guidance and to have faith that we were right were we needed to be. We also realized that taking a leap of faith is not always easy, but once you've jumped, your life is never the same.

chapter

12

More Than Just a Message

Over the past eleven chapters you've read numerous accounts of spirit coming forward to communicate messages from the other side. You've read stories of children reconnecting with their parents, spouses sharing messages of love, and even a cat who came to let his owner know he's still around. Spirit's message of love and hope is a profound one, but what does it ultimately mean for us here in the physical world? If we know that spirit lives on, what does that mean for us now, here in this moment?

As a medium, my mentors always told me that mediumship is more than just a message. That spirit communication calls us to look more deeply into our own existence and the nature of our spirit. With new advances in science and quantum physics today, the mysteries of the universe and the understanding of self are beginning to be unraveled. In the dramatic times we live in, there is a call for a deeper understanding of why we are here and what our purpose is. To connect with spirit is to know that the veil between the two worlds is very thin, and our connection to our loved ones and those around us is very close.

We play a role in one another's lives. Our connection is a delicate dance, and we float in and out of experiences and circumstances impacting and assisting each other in our souls' development on Earth. Our loved ones in spirit also reach out and participate in this dance, guiding us as we continue this journey. In communicating with our loved ones, we come from a place of either love or fear—when we choose love, we choose the true essence of our soul, and anything becomes possible.

When you feel that connection to the source, you know with every ounce of your soul that there is more than just this physical incarnation. You come to realize that you truly are a spiritual being having a physical experience. Life becomes a delightful journey full of joy and wonder. Even in the face of disbelief or skepticism, it is possible to find common ground; it is possible to unite on a human-to-human level. When I was growing up, for example, my friend Doug and I had numerous debates about the afterlife and the existence of a soul. As an atheist, he believed there is nothing after death; as a medium, my experience has shown me there is more.

Our debate went on for years, until one day we both realized that neither of us were going to change our minds about the afterlife. However, what we could agree upon was how we could work together to make this moment of now, this moment here in the physical, a better place. We understood that what connected us as human beings was more important than the differences in our afterlife philosophies. This bond, this connection and common ground, is a liberating experience. It becomes no longer about you and me, but about us—humanity and the world.

However, this awareness of all being *one* can be lost when grief over the death of a friend or family member is so heavy and so unbearable that the meaning of life seems to vanish from our experience. In that grief, we may experience a loss in faith, a fear of the unknown, and a sense of hopelessness. In those moments, it is so very important to reach out to others who can help you, who can remind you that you are not alone in your experience. In part, this is what mediumship does. When a medium is able to help two souls connect again, it can provide a sense of relief, peace, and healing that may not have come otherwise.

In my years of offering my services as a medium, it is the letters and responses from individuals who have been touched by the experience of communication that have inspired me the most. One of the most touching letters I've received came from a woman named Carol, who had lost her twenty-six-year-old son, Jon, to colon cancer. She had been grief-stricken since his passing, and, although she was a woman of strong faith, her faith had begun to falter as she tried to figure out how she could move forward without her son.

When I met Carol for the first time, I was unaware that it was her son who she wanted to hear from, but as his communication came forward, it was clear to her that his spirit lived on. Following the session, Carol wrote me a letter:

My Dearest Troy,

I want you to know that you helped me get out of the deepest, lowest hole I think a person can ever endure. Jon's loss is filled with so much heartache for hundreds of people. He made such an impact on all ages. In his eighteen months of a painful, monster illness he never complained or asked why; instead, he said 'why not?' He always put everyone first ... On a website that hosted his story, in four months he had thirty thousand hits from all he affected! You can see what a unique spirit he was and is!! He had just finished college and wanted so much to help people and make a difference in this world ... It looks like he is fulfilling his dream in the spirit world. I will be eternally grateful that God led me to Laura, who introduced me to you, and I am most grateful and blessed to have you in my life. A miracle has happened to me ... I finally have some sort of comfort and peace in this gut-wrenching loss of my only beloved son ... you are a treasure to cherish!!!!!!!!

Love,

Carol

As a medium, but more importantly as a human being, it is my mission to be a bridge for people, whether they are here in the physical or on the other side. My calling to continue this work comes from this place of service. Being in service to others is where miracles occur—where ego falls away, and the pure natural instinct to help and support your fellow neighbor comes through.

So what does all of this mean? I believe spirit communication provides us with an opportunity to recognize how precious every moment of communication is with our loved ones. People often tell me how much they savor those moments of communication with their loved ones who come forward through my work. They comment on how the thing they long for the most is just the opportunity to talk with their loved one again, even if just for a moment. The power of this work is to remind people that the precious moment to connect is also occurring right now—with their loved ones and friends who are *alive.*

What would you say to your mom or your best friend if you knew you wouldn't see them again tomorrow? To be conscious, to be aware, to live in the present moment with everyone is an incredible experience to strive for. Sure, it may be difficult to be present in every moment, but the joy of being there makes the effort worthwhile. If you really want to experience the beauty and the joy of the present moment with friends and family, I encourage you to try this exercise:

> The next time you are together at a birthday party or a holiday, imagine that your loved ones who have passed away are at that party. Feel that sense of longing and that desire to be connected with their energy. Once you've recognized the desire to re-experience those moments with a lost loved one, realize that years down the road you will have this feeling for the people you are with right *now*, and they will have this desire for you. This subtle awareness can shift your experience in that moment and provide an enhanced sense of gratitude and joy.

In that moment, all five senses will be energized: your food will taste more flavorful, you'll smell all the delicious fragrances, the sounds around you will be fine-tuned, your sense of touch will be intensified, and you will see the experience through a new set of eyes. With your five senses enhanced, you'll also open up to your sixth sense, where you'll discover that the loved ones you were wishing were there, are in fact there in spirit. You will sense them, hear them, or smell them.

Nature has shown us that there are cycles and seasons to everything. What blossoms in the spring, grows and dies and returns again the next year. On a quantum level, we are energy, and you cannot destroy or kill energy—it will just transform into another form of itself. Through spirit communication, we can be reassured that our souls live on and our connection to our loved ones never dies.

chapter

13

The Media and Mediumship

Ever since I was a kid, I've always enjoyed movies. There is some-thing exciting about being able to lose yourself in a film, living vicariously through the characters on the screen. With the advent of home video cameras in the 1990s, I found myself making short movies with my friends and doing my best to make the next epic film on our no-budget production. Ultimately, of course, I chose to pursue my dream of becoming a filmmaker and received my undergrad degree in film production. There is something so enticing and rewarding about bringing something to the screen that had previously existed only in your mind.

In the early years of my development as a medium, *The Sixth Sense* was released. This film about a young boy who "sees dead people" was a box office success, and the subject of spirit communication became the next Hollywood hot topic. Other films soon followed, and eventually TV made its way to the other side with Sci-Fi's *Crossing Over with John Edward*, NBC's *Medium*, and, finally, CBS's *The Ghost Whisperer*. As a filmmaker, I loved these programs. All of the technical details of the productions were incredible. The writing, the cinematography, and the acting in these scripted shows all made for very well-done programs.

While as a viewer I couldn't help but be drawn into the characters and the twists and turns of the story, as a medium I had some moments of uneasiness. It was occasionally disappointing to see how violent and scary the experience was for the characters of the mediums. In some depictions, the mediums almost seemed like victims to the communication, and I was always curious about why the experience had to be portrayed in such a dark way. Of course, as a filmmaker and producer I completely understood the need to create drama and fear—those elements are what put butts in the seats or get people to tune in.

It's strange balancing between two worlds when it comes to filmmaking and mediumship. There are times when I feel that the media represents mediumship well, and then there are times where I think it sensationalizes the process. I'm sure every occupation ever represented in the movies says, "That's not how it would happen in real life." I'm sure there are astronauts who would say some of the space films are far-fetched, or tornado hunters who would claim that Bill Paxton and Helen Hunt would never survive in the middle of a tornado. But I do tip my hat to the film and television industry for continuing to keep the topic of spirit communication in the public eye.

Since I'm both a filmmaker and a medium, people often ask me which films I like or would recommend about spirit communication and the afterlife. While there are a number of movies that highlight spirit communication in realistic ways, my four favorite films (or scenes from films) that depict how mediumship and spirit communication work in the "real world" are *Field of Dreams, What Dreams May Come, Ghost,* and *The Sixth Sense.*

Field of Dreams

This Oscar-nominated film, from 1989, follows the story of Iowa farmer Ray Kinsella (Kevin Costner) who hears a voice in his cornfield that tells him, "If you build it, he will come." Inspired, yet unsure of who is speaking or where the voice is coming from, Ray follows the instruction and builds a baseball diamond in his cornfield. The spirits of the 1919 Chicago White Sox baseball players subsequently appear on the field and begin to play. When the voices continue and further messages of inspiration come, Ray's journey takes him to Boston and back as he tries to understand what it all means.

This is an extraordinary film on many levels, but the area I wish to focus on is the scene in which Ray hears the voice telling him, "If you build it, he will come." He is working in his cornfield when he hears the voice. After having heard it a few times already and questioning his own sanity, Ray hears the voice yet again: "If you build it, he will come." This time Ray tries to confront the voice. As he looks around the cornfield, he has a vision of the baseball diamond he will build there and sees the image of Shoeless Joe Jackson.

When Ray realizes what the voice is requesting and what he is being called to do, he shares his vision with his wife Annie (Amy Madigan). Annie's first reaction is that Ray is crazy, but as he continues to share why he's being called to build the field, Annie becomes enthralled by what he sees. When Ray point-blank asks her, "Do you think I'm crazy?" Annie responds, "Yes … but I also think if you really feel you should do this, you should do it."

What's most compelling about this scene is Ray's willingness to embrace what he is called to do, even in the face of fear. As a medium or intuitive, when voices from spirit come—whether they are the voices of loved ones, spirit guides, your own higher self, or God—coming to a space of trust in what you're receiving is the most challenging part. Yes, you may do a double take and have moments of doubt, but it is the indescribable pull to follow that inspiration that can transform our lives. It's in that moment—when we choose to follow our heart, to follow our soul—that we remember who we are and why we are here.

Annie's support for Ray should also be recognized. In doing this, she becomes a cocreator in the process; all the magic and the miracles that follow would not have occurred without her. This is an extraordinary example of how the friends and family in our lives support our calling and support our visions. In my own life, the commitment and support I received from my wife Chanda is what helped me embrace my calling. Chanda's belief in me gave me the confidence to trust in my role as a medium and to recognize that the messages coming from spirit were not something I should hide from, but something I should share with the world.

I have seen *Field of Dreams* more times than I can count. I've even visited the baseball diamond in Dyersville, Iowa, where they shot the film. There is a magic and an energy in this movie that inspires and motivates you to follow your heart and your dreams. So next time you hear a voice that inspires you, choose to listen ... and see what adventure unfolds in your life.

What Dreams May Come

This visually stunning film about the afterlife, produced in 1998, was based on Richard Matheson's 1978 novel *What Dreams May Come*. The movie follows the story of Chris Nielson (Robin Williams), a doctor whose two children die in a car crash; he dies in an accident himself a few years later. When his widow Annie (Annabella Sciorra) takes her own life, Chris crosses heaven and hell to reunite with his wife and soul mate. When I first saw the trailer for this film, I was mesmerized. I just couldn't wait for it to be released in theaters, so I immediately ordered the book and read the story first.

The novel *What Dreams May Come* transformed my perspective on death and provided an incredible narrative on the journey into the afterlife. In his introductory note, Matheson explains that the characters are the only fictional component of the book. Almost everything else is based on research, and, at the end of the novel, he includes a lengthy bibliography.

As a medium, there is one scene in the film that I believe is a wonderful representation of how our loved ones reach out to us and we sometimes don't allow their message in. After the character of Chris dies, his spirit visits his wife, who is dealing with an unbearable amount of grief. As Annie is writing in her journal, she begins to sense Chris' presence. Chris' spirit draws close to her hand, and he begins to motion and to repeat, "This is Chris, I still exist." Annie's hand moves across the paper and in a very rough form of automatic writing (in which spirit moves or inspires the writer's hand to move), Annie writes on her paper, *This is Chris, I still exist.* However, Annie cannot let the message in, and the link to Chris is lost as she screams, tears up the paper, and returns to her grief.

This scene is very powerful. The realization that Chris' messages are getting through provides hope for the viewer and for Annie, but that joy only lasts a few moments since Annie refuses to believe what is written. As a medium, I believe this scene represents what it can be like for our loved ones in spirit when they reach out to us. They so badly want us to know that they still exist; however, in our grief and resistance we may not be able to allow their communication in.

Trust is the key theme here, again. Annie is not able to trust the impressions she is receiving, and, as a result, she loses out on a beautiful connection with the spirit of her husband. As mediums or intuitives, trust is the most important aspect of the work. If you cannot trust your intuition and the messages you are receiving, you cannot be a clear channel for spirit. Yes, this trust may take some time and the messages may not come overnight, but they do come. And when they do, there is indescribable joy and freedom of knowing that your loved one is with you and does still exist.

Ghost

One of the best known films about spirit communication is the 1990 movie *Ghost*. This dramatic love story follows Sam Wheat (Patrick Swayze), a New York banker who is murdered during a botched mugging. Sam's love for his girlfriend Molly (Demi Moore), and his desire to keep her safe, enables his soul to remain on Earth as a ghost. He communicates with Molly through psychic medium Oda Mae Brown (Whoopi Goldberg, who won an Oscar for her role), helping Molly to stay alive and solve his murder.

There are so many things about this film that I love. First of all, there are a number of scenes depicting spirit communication as it tends to actually occur for mediums. The first time that Sam communicates with Oda Mae, we see that the medium has to start trusting her abilities. What also makes the film realistic is Oda Mae's ability to hear Sam, but not see him. Oda Mae discovers that clairaudience (clear hearing) is her strongest ability; this illustrates that not all mediums see spirit—some only hear or sense them.

The core message in the film is that love doesn't die, that love is something you take with you. And although Sam and Molly are no longer connected in the physical, their love connects them in spirit. Oda Mae also transforms from a psychic fraud into a spiritual messenger. Her ability to help Sam connect with Molly opens the door to others in spirit who wish to share their message. When you come from a place of love and service, anything is possible. *Ghost* is a movie that always inspires me; for me as a medium, it represents the true beauty and purpose of spirit communication.

The Sixth Sense

This well-crafted film, from director M. Night Shyamalan, follows the story of a child psychologist (Bruce Willis) who helps a young boy named Cole Sear (Haley Joel Osment) come to terms with his ability to see spirits. It is also the film that catapulted the phrase "I see dead people" into pop culture.

As a filmmaker, I loved this film. It was well shot, well acted, and incredibly well written—with a twist at the end that still has people talking. As a medium, though, I have mixed feelings. The movie was marketed as a thriller, and most of the film portrays Cole's abilities to see dead people as a scary, uncontrollable experience. The tagline of the film even declared, "Not every gift is a blessing." I find this disappointing because it implies that connecting with the afterlife will be a scary experience, when in fact it never has to be. However, despite Cole's initial negative encounters with spirit, he experiences a positive shift when he comes to understand that he can help people with his gift. This recognition—of his ability to be of service—reveals the true power of spirit communication.

One of the most compelling scenes in the film, and, in my opinion, one of the best representations of the beauty and the healing power of spirit communication, comes near the end when Cole shares his gift with his mother Lynn (Toni Collette) for the first time. While the two are stuck in traffic, Cole relays a message from spirit. He connects with his maternal grandmother and is able to tell his mother that her mother was able to see her in a dance recital as a child.

The grandmother is also able to answer one of Lynn's questions. Lynn had visited her mother's grave a number of times and had asked, "Do I make you proud?" Cole is able to tell his mother that Grandma's answer was "every day." It is a tear-filled moment for both mother and son, but the healing and understanding that comes for Cole and Lynn represents the healing and purpose behind spirit communication. The messages from spirit are not meant to "wow" or "amaze"; they are here to comfort and heal. Every time I watch this moment in the film, I get a lump in my throat and my eyes water, since I know how this scene represents the incredible power of communicating with spirit.

· · ·

It's films like these that I am committed to making as a filmmaker and a medium—films that move, touch, and inspire the people who are watching. As a result, I have been drawn to the films of Stephen Simon. Stephen is the Hollywood producer who brought *Somewhere in Time* and *What Dreams May Come* to the screen. Stephen also became the founding father of the Spiritual Cinema movement; he wrote the bible on Spiritual Cinema, which is called *The Force Is With You: Mystical Movie Messages That Inspire Our Lives.* He also produced and directed the film version of one of my favorite books, *Conversations with God.*

My initial desire to connect and work with Stephen occurred when I saw *What Dreams May Come.* Only a few short years later, I actually had the opportunity to meet Stephen at the Edge Life Expo in Minneapolis. This premiere holistic and metaphysical expo brings in a number of inspiring speakers each year and, in 2002, I had the opportunity to hear Stephen speak and meet him face-to-face. It was a true pleasure to meet a producer who was committed to creating spiritually themed, uplifting movies that ask the questions "Who are we?" and "Why are we here?"

My connection to Stephen continued over the next few years. I took his mystical movie telecourses and helped organize local screenings of spiritually themed films through his Spiritual Cinema Network and his Spiritual Cinema Circle, a monthly DVD club that distributes such films. From the moment I met Stephen, I knew that I wanted to bring him to Fargo so he could share his message with the community. Fargo is home to a beautiful, historic movie house called the Fargo Theatre. This 870-seat, art-deco theater was listed as one of the "10 great places to revel in cinematic grandeur" by *USA Today*. It is home to the annual Fargo Film Festival and was the location for the screening of some of Stephen's spiritual films.

My first attempt to bring Stephen to Fargo occurred in 2003, when he released his directorial debut *Indigo*, a narrative film about a young girl with psychic abilities. The girl is part of a new generation of children, born with enhanced awareness or other healing gifts, called Indigo children. The intent was to have Stephen present his film at the 2003 Fargo Film Festival. However, plans fell through and Stephen was not able to make it to Fargo. It was a disappointment at the time, as I so badly wanted to share Stephen with our community, but I understood that he would make his way to Fargo when the time was right. I held on to the vision for another five years and, in 2008, through the help of the Fargo Holistic Expo and a number of sponsors in the Fargo-Moorhead area, Stephen came to Fargo and shared his message of uplifting films with our community.

Stephen's visit was a dream come true for me. His work and message was something that had inspired me for years, and it was a pleasure to be able to help bring that message to the community where I was raised. For Stephen, the experience was a very sacred one. He had been raised in a Hollywood family and grew up in the classic Hollywood film industry, and so immediately fell in love with the Historic Fargo Theatre. He was incredibly grateful to have had the experience to present in that jewel of a movie house in Fargo.

Even though having Stephen visit Fargo was a wonderful gift and an example of what five years of patience and persistence can manifest, the most profound gift Stephen gave was creating a space for me to declare that I am both a medium and a filmmaker. It was through his Spiritual Cinema telecourses back in 2002–2003 that I was able to share with other filmmakers that I was also a medium. Previously, I had never spoken of the two things in the same sentence, since I was concerned about looking crazy. But Stephen's stance in support of Spiritual Cinema as a viable genre opened the door for me to fully share with the world who I am. I am eternally grateful to Stephen for creating this space. In retrospect, I never thought Stephen's mentoring would have anything to do with my mediumship. But now I truly see how I can be both a filmmaker and a medium.

Through the years, I've created short documentary films, produced a twenty-six-episode television series on natural childbirth and midwifery for Discovery Health Channel, and searched for a number of "monsters" for a History Channel television series. Through it all, I realize that spirit is leading the way. I never thought that I could live in Fargo, North Dakota, and be both a filmmaker and a medium. I believe it goes to show that it doesn't matter where you live—you can still impact the world. And if I can do it in Fargo, I can do it anywhere. As the next phase of my life continues, I'm excited to see where spirit will lead me.

So, fade to black. That's a wrap for this chapter.

14

Developing Your Own Abilities

If I know anything to be true about mediumship, it is this: it's not just for the gifted, and it's an ability we all have access to. How do I know that? Because I never thought it was something that was possible for me. However, through my own development and my own study, I strengthened my intuitive muscle, which is what brought me to where I am today. I like to think of it like basketball. On some level, we all have the ability to pick up a ball and throw it through the net. For some of us, that's merely crumpling up a piece of paper and tossing it in the trash can; for others, it's playing basketball in high school; and yet there are others who are playing in professional games every night. We all have the abilities—it's just how we choose to develop them.

The intent of this chapter is to provide you with some basics for mediumship development, in order to help you take a solid step forward in this exciting study. I see personal development falling into three basic areas: reading, development classes/mentoring, and practical experience. The important thing to remember is that you never suddenly "arrive" at being a medium. Mediumship, like any ability, is something that continues to evolve and grow as you practice. Just as golfers can always hone their game and are only as good as their last drive or putt, a medium can and will always continue to learn and grow, developing their abilities.

Reading

To begin your development as a medium, the best place to start is with books. Reading the life stories of other mediums is a very helpful process, in that you learn what they went through in their own development. Books on the historical development of mediumship are also helpful. Having a strong foundation in the history, techniques, and dynamics of the field of mediumship is a very important aspect for effective communications. (I've included a list of recommended readings at the back of the book to help you on your journey.)

It's also important to remember that you can find a lot of valuable information on the Internet as well. Yes, you still have to use your own discernment about what resonates with you and what doesn't, but the web can be a great source for information and also expand your community, allowing you to reach out to other mediums or like-minded people through blogs, social networking groups, or email lists. My own journey wouldn't have been possible without the Internet. I believe spirit was guiding me that day I found the First Spiritual Temple online.

Development Classes/Mentoring

When I began my study of mediumship in Boston I was fortunate to study in a proper mediumship development circle. A mediumship development circle is a group of people who come together once a week at the same time to develop their abilities as mediums. Development circles are an invaluable resource because they give you the safety and support of working with a group of like-minded people. In addition, the collective intent of the group can, in some instances, help enhance your abilities more quickly than if you were trying to develop your abilities on your own. But if an official development circle is not something you have access to, you can create such a circle on your own.

Finding a mentor is also an important aspect of mediumship development. A mentor can provide the insight and structure you may need to develop your abilities. Mentors are also there to help you recognize what is working and what isn't. Finding an individual who has worked as a medium or intuitive, at present or in the past, is a good start. Mentors are there to help you understand how the process works and to give you the strength to keep moving forward.

Practical Experience

Nothing helps you develop your work as a medium more than practice, practice, and practice. The more often you can give messages from spirit, the better you will become. It's important to start off by giving messages to friends and family. Their support and love will help provide a safe buffer as you begin to understand how the communication comes forward. Once you begin to practice and your friends and family tell others about your success, you will get the opportunity to increase your abilities by working with new people.

One of the most important things to remember in your development is to never give unsolicited messages. When I began my development I felt spirit close by quite often. There were moments I'd be on the subway and begin to see spirits around someone I was sitting next to. My mentors had always stressed how important it is not to approach a stranger and say, "Oh, excuse me, sir. I have a grandma here who would like to say hello." This kind of communication can rock somebody's foundation, and if they react in a negative light, it can put all of you in an awkward situation. It's always important to ask permission from a person first, before you offer them a reading.

So, remember to start with people who support your new journey, and work your way toward more people from there.

Spirit Communication 101

To help provide a little more clarity on the process of spirit communication and how it works, I feel it's first important to emphasize the difference between a medium and a psychic. A psychic is an individual who can sense information about a person, place, or thing. They connect with individuals on a one-to-one level. A medium is an individual who is able to sense communication from another individual in spirit and is able to relay their message. Thus, when a medium is involved, a triangular connection is formed: the medium, the spirit, and the person receiving the message. All mediums are psychic, but psychics aren't necessarily mediumistic.

Spirit communication tends to come in one of three ways: clairvoyance (clear seeing), clairsentience (clear sensing), and clairaudience (clear hearing). There are also other, less common "clairs," such as claircognizance (clear knowing), clairalience (clear smelling), and clairgustance (clear tasting). It's also important to remember that these senses are within the intuitive realm and may not be something you actual see, hear, or feel in the physical world. When it comes to "seeing" spirit, I like to tell people it's kind of like picturing someone standing next to you. You can imagine the person standing there, but you don't necessarily see them as physically as you see the chair. Now, there may be some people who are able to see spirit that clearly, but in most instances it is a communication that comes from within the mind's eye. As you develop, it's also important to remember that you may not use all three main senses in your work. You may see better than you hear, or you may sense more than you see, or you may experience a combination of all three.

If you choose to develop or explore your own intuitive or mediumistic abilities, it's good to realize that you are not alone in the process. There are spirits on the other side who are actually assisting you in your development. These individuals are known as spirit guides. A spirit guide is an individual in spirit who works directly with you on your development in this lifetime. They are with you from birth to death, and whether you are aware of them or not, they are there to assist you and inspire you upon your path. I like to think of a guide like Jiminy Cricket on your shoulder or a guardian angel. There are many perspectives and writings on spirit guides and angels. Some people see them as two separate entities, but in this instance, whether you call this support your spirit guide or your angel, it's more important to just know that there is a special spirit there for you.

It's also valuable to know that you never *need* a medium or a psychic. Although it can be a powerful experience to receive verifiable information from a complete stranger, it's more important to remember that you can receive communication from your loved ones through your own abilities at any time. Oftentimes it just takes a few moments of silence to help the process. Remember that communication can come through dreams, songs, signs, scents, feelings, and a number of other ways. It's helpful to first look for a logical explanation for what you perceive—for example, if you feel a cool breeze on your neck, check to see if the window is open. If the window is not open and you feel at the pit of your soul that it was communication, then trust your impressions and accept it as a message from spirit. I often say that if you experience three or more "coincidences," then God is trying to tell you something. If you receive more than three signs from a loved one, trust it!

Personal discernment is one of the most challenging aspects in the development of your intuitive abilities. How do you know what's communication from spirit and what might be your own hopes and desires? Ultimately, the way to distinguish between these is to practice. The more you work with receiving spirit's message, the more you will understand what is what. Spirit communication can occur in very subtle ways, and having patience in developing the process and patience with those in spirit around you will help tremendously. Also, be clear as to what your intentions are with your development. Mediumship is not a parlor game or a neat trick to try on friends. It's a very serious endeavor and should be presented and treated as such. If you are able to realize that spirit is coming forward to you to relay a message to someone, it may be the only opportunity this spirit has to share what he or she needs to communicate. Approach this work with integrity and love.

The quickest way to begin the process of connecting with spirit is to sit for meditation. Now, stop, don't run away ... meditation isn't something that has to be a difficult or laborious process. Nor do you have to sit with your legs crossed and say "om" to yourself for an hour. Meditation can be as simple as taking a few moments to pause in your hectic day and just quiet your mind. Being mindful of your breath and allowing slow deep breaths in and out can help open your mind to new insights and inspiration. Meditation can also be a wonderful way for you to reach out and connect with your loved ones in spirit. Below, you will find a sample meditation I offer to people to help them connect with their loved ones in spirit.

Connecting with Your Loved Ones in Spirit

Take a few moments now to relax. And with each breath in and out I want you to imagine that you are expanding your light, you are expanding your soul. As you take this moment to center yourself and focus on your breath, you become like a beacon of light, shining brightly so that those in spirit can draw closer to you. Just take these next few moments here to find that place of peace, to find that place of connection.

As you become relaxed, I want you to invite someone to come to you. Someone you are hoping to hear from, someone you have perhaps been missing—a loved one, a family member, a friend who is now on the other side. Invite them to draw close to you; imagine them standing in front of you. And as you do so, it's important to remember and to acknowledge the things that you are seeing, hearing, and sensing.

You don't need a medium or a psychic to connect to your loved ones in spirit; it is an ability we all have and is a connection that we can all make. So as you find yourself now in this moment of silence, send out that invitation and invite that person you are hoping to connect with close to you. And as you begin to build this link, allow the emotion, allow the feelings, and allow the connection. See that person, hear that person, feel that person, for they are still here. They are still present. They are still connected.

Take these next few moments now just to be in their space, in connection with them. Feel free to ask them questions or share your thoughts. And then sit quietly and trust the impressions you have received. You have built this bridge between two worlds.

And you are connected to the loved one you wished to reach. Be, together, in the space of communication...

Meditation is a wonderful process. It can be quite powerful not only in connecting you to your loved ones, but also helping you manage the stress of everyday life. So whether you choose to sit on the top of a mountain or in your own backyard, meditation allows you to reconnect to your own spirit—so that you can connect to the spirit that connects us all.

chapter

15

It's a Journey, Not a Destination

So where do we go from here? It's a question that comes up for me every morning when I wake up. Where am I going and why? And more importantly, when will I get there? As a medium, I've discovered that my development and the study of all things spiritual is a lifelong process. It's not something that occurs overnight. As much as I'd like to have all the insight and awareness now, it doesn't happen that way. My mentors always reminded me that with time comes wisdom. When I first started out, the thought of being ten years down the road in my mediumship development seemed like an eternity. Now that I'm ten years into my development, I realize that a decade can fly by quickly.

The road that lies ahead of me is an exciting one. In the next ten years there will be more learning, more messages, and, with any luck, more wisdom. Stepping into this calling hasn't always been easy for me. However, the messages of hope and healing that I've delivered over the years are something that continue to inspire me daily. Those messages have also reminded me how precious this life experience is, how every moment counts, and the opportunity to be a fully conscious spirit in a physical body is what brings heaven to Earth *now*, right in this moment. To know that our souls live on is to know that love never dies. To remember that our souls live on also allows us to embrace who we truly are. In this space of remembrance, miracles manifest.

When I was in high school, I used to carry around a little laminated quote in my pocket. It is a statement that inspires me to this day. As this book comes to an end, I leave you with this message, that it might help you on your journey and remind you each day of how beautiful life is. Share it with your loved ones, share it with your family, share it with the world, so that you make the connection here and now with those you love, and not wait until after they have passed.

> *Live each day to the fullest. Get the most from each hour, each day, and each age of your life. Then you can look forward with confidence, and back without regrets.*
>
> *Be yourself, but be your best self. Dare to be different and to follow your own star.*
>
> *And don't be afraid to be happy. Enjoy what is beautiful. Love with all your heart and soul. Believe that those you love, love you.*
>
> *Forget what you have done for your friends, and remember what they have done for you. Disregard what the world owes you, and concentrate on what you owe the world.*

When you are faced with a decision, make that decision wisely as possible then forget it. The moment of absolute certainty never arrives.

And above all, remember that God helps those who help themselves. Act as if everything depended upon you, and pray as if everything depended upon God.

—S. H. Payer

Thank you for sharing your time with me and for allowing me to share my journey with you. May it remind you of how precious and magical your bond to spirit truly is.

Epilogue: The Dandelion

Over the years of sharing my work and offering my services as a medium, I've witnessed many incredible and inspiring things. This book has highlighted some of my favorite stories and experiences. Oftentimes, people ask me if I'm still surprised by the powerful messages and symbols I receive that demonstrate soul's survival—and my answer is, absolutely yes!

And I continue to be amazed by the signs of support for my own journey. The creation of this book, in fact, was accompanied by a number of unique signs or coincidences. For example, I discussed a number of different title options with my publisher, ultimately choosing *Bridge to the Afterlife*. The word "bridge" and the symbolism of a bridge is very poignant to me, because it is the same symbolism I used when I first went public with my work. I used the bridge theme on my business cards, and my first email even contained the word "bridge." To see it come back again somehow feels right. I see how many things in my journey have now come full circle.

Even more remarkable are the signs I experienced regarding my book's front cover. In book publishing, the cover design can be created in a number of different ways. If you self-publish, you may end up designing the cover yourself or hiring someone; when you have a publisher, as I did with Llewellyn, there is an in-house designer who creates the look. Given my background in advertising and film, I was very excited to see what the team at Llewellyn had in store. And what I saw confirmed just how powerful spirit's signs can be.

After the title of the book was selected, my editor and I shared some initial thoughts with the cover designer. A month or so went by, and then I received the design via email. I must admit that I was a bit surprised when I first opened the file. I wasn't expecting to see a dandelion. I thought there would be, literally, a picture of a bridge on the cover. But as I continued to look at the design, I thought that there was something very familiar about the image. Then, like a bolt of lightning, it hit me ... I had seen this image before, and not in a picture. I had looked at a dandelion, from this exact angle, on a walk just the week before.

One of my morning routines when the weather is nice is to go for a walk near my home. I often listen to music and take moments along my stroll to stop and observe Mother Nature from various perspectives. I crawl under trees and see what things look like from that angle. I get close to a leaf and see how the veins create a beautiful design, and I stop and lie down on my stomach to get a low-angle view of dandelions across the grass, the sky behind them. When my wife Chanda and I were out walking, that week before the cover design arrived, I had in fact stopped her and pulled her to the ground to observe the beauty of a dandelion that had frost on it. We looked at it from the exact same angle that it now appears on my book.

When I showed Chanda the cover and reminded her of our walk, she couldn't help but think it was a sign. As cool as I thought it was, though, there was still part of me that thought maybe it was just a coincidence. Despite what I do, I still tend to be a bit skeptical; even though I tell my clients to watch for signs, I sometimes forget to do it myself. Luckily the universe seems to understand that I have this bit of skepticism, so it tends to give me more than one sign to show that it's not just a coincidence. As I like to say, "Three or more signs, and God is trying to tell you something."

So, with one sign down, I waited to see if signs two and three would come along. They did, of course, although I wasn't quite prepared for how they would come.

Sign two came about a month after I'd first seen the cover, when I showed the design to my good friend Sheri. (I tell Sheri's story, and about the passing of her partner Peg, in chapter 10.) Well, when Sheri saw the design, she thought it was beautiful. She also laughed and said, "How's that for a sign, huh?"

I was a bit confused by her comment, since I hadn't told her about how I'd seen a dandelion from this angle. "What sign are you referring to?" I asked.

"Don't you remember?" she responded. "During the last few weeks of Peg's life, you shared a message with her from spirit. In the message, spirit compared Peg to a dandelion that has gone to seed. The wind comes up and scatters the seeds everywhere, regardless of whether the seeds land on fertile ground or hard soil. Her wisdom, ideas, and generous spirit were shared equally with all. She had so much to share with others, and she was very generous with her knowledge. You said that if Peg were a flower, she'd be a dandelion."

I couldn't believe what I was hearing. I had completely forgotten about that message, but Peg's spirit was letting herself be known again through the imagery of my cover design. The thought that Peg may have been close to the designer as he was putting the images together warmed my heart. It reminded me that Peg is with me—she is still here.

Quite frankly, after that I was sold on the design! I knew that these were two very big coincidences, and therefore they weren't just coincidences—it was the universe's and Peg's way of letting me know I was on the right track. It still floors me to think about it! It just seems like a million-to-one chance that the designer would be inspired to use a dandelion for the cover when the dandelion had such a strong connection for me.

After those two solid connections, I was curious to see where number three would come from. It wasn't long afterwards that I came across some information that would seal the deal. In my research on dandelions, I learned about the metaphysical symbolism for the flower. And guess what ... dandelions are symbolic for divination, wishes, and calling spirits. I don't think it can be any more clear than that.

Three signs, one powerful message ... so yes, I'm still amazed by the ways spirit will get a message across. Sometimes the symbols are subtle, sometimes they take a little while to see, but they are there and they do exist. So be sure to keep your eyes, ears, and senses open. Your sign is just around the corner.

Acknowledgments

When you reflect back on thirty years of your life while writing an autobiography, you can't help but be humbled by all the people who played an important part in creating who you are today. For all the people who played this role in my life, I am eternally grateful. And for those who played a role in my journey as a medium, here are my thanks to you.

To God, the Universe, the Higher Power, or the Source: The greatest joy in life is feeling the oneness of God and knowing how everything is truly interconnected. I'm so grateful that I remembered our connection at such a young age.

To my spirit guides and workers: Your patience and inspiration is priceless. Thank you for being that silent guiding force in my life and work as a medium.

To Rev. Simeon, Rev. Stephen, Syrsha, Mr. Ayer, Crystal, and my friends and classmates at the First Spiritual Temple: I would not be where I am today without your guidance, mentoring, and support.

To my wife and soul mate, Chanda: Your support and persistence in seeing me continue to build my connection to spirit is incredible. I can't imagine being here without you. And the absolute best part of this journey for me is seeing you develop your own gifts. Your one-of-a-kind way with spirit touches and transforms so many lives. You are my best teacher, and I learn from you every day. I love you.

To my son, Jacob: Your little spirit has taught me so much in the five years you've been on this earth. You help me understand how powerful love can be between a child and a parent.

To my family and friends: To Mom and Darwin, Dad and Mary, Shawn, Heidi, and Megan, and their families; to Andy, Sara, and Karla, and their families; to all the Parkinsons, Wittmiers, Cinks, and Weyers; also to my in-laws, the Schnaibles. Thank you all for your love and support. *To members of the Fearsome Fivesome:* Doug Ficek, Reed Sigmund, Timm Sharp, and Jason AC Spencer. Thanks for the laughs and the love. You guys are my other soul mates!

To all those in the production world: From natural childbirth to searching for Bigfoot to all the people that knew me first as "Troy the Filmmaker," I appreciate your friendship and support. To Stephen Simon, thank you for being a pioneer in the spiritual cinema genre. Your mentoring and support through the years has been priceless.

To the Spiritual Communities of Fargo-Moorhead, Froggy 99.9 FM, and the Edge Life Holistic Journal: Thank you for letting me share my abilities. From the *A Course in Miracles* gang to the Master Mind groups, there is nothing stronger than a community who can share in a conscious conversation. To the morning gang at Froggy, thank you for the invitation to share messages on your station—I don't think you truly realize how many listeners you touch. To Gary, Insiah, and the team at the Edge Life Group, your support and partnership has opened so many wonderful doors.

To the handful of people who have helped make this book possible: To Lesley Bolton, for your friendship and editor's eye on the book's proposal; to Carrie Obry and the team at Llewellyn, for believing I had a story to share; to Sharon Staton, for your early support; to Michael McAllister, for the space to write; to Jason and Stacey Roth, for your support and your space; to the Harvalas, who became our second family; to Miata Edoga, for your coaching and guidance before we took the leap; to Laura Egland, for your second set of eyes; to Sheri Woxland—so much to say, so little room—always remember you were the first T.W.I.L.A.! And to Landis, for being a catalyst in this process and for opening your home to us in Hawaii. You showed us what's possible in this world.

To the individuals and families I have sat with through the years: Thank you for sharing your family members in spirit with me. I have learned so much from your mothers, fathers, brothers, sisters, children, grandparents, and friends. Thank you to all of those in spirit I have connected with. You are truly some of my greatest teachers.

Lastly, I'd like to thank my *Grandpa and Grandma Parkinson.* You were the first grandparents in my life to pass away, and thus you became my motivation for exploring mediumship. Thank you for making your presence known to me, and thank you for playing a pivotal role in my spiritual journey.

Recommended Resources

On Your Spiritual Journey

Brinkley, Dannion. *Saved by the Light*. New York: HarperOne, 2008.

A Course in Miracles. Mill Valley, CA: Foundation for Inner Peace, 1992.

Eadie, Betty J. *Embraced by the Light*. Placerville, CA: Gold Leaf Press, 1992.

Matheson, Richard. *What Dreams May Come*. New York: Tor Books, 1978.

Simon, Stephen. *The Force Is With You: Mystical Movie Messages That Inspire Our Lives*. Charlottesville, VA: Hampton Roads Publishing, 2002.

Walsch, Neale Donald. *Conversations with God*. 3 vol. New York: Putnam Adult, 1996.

Weiss, Brian. *Many Lives, Many Masters*. New York: Fireside, 1988.

Zukav, Gary. *Seat of the Soul*. New York: Fireside, 1989.

On Your Spirit Communication Exploration

Berkowitz, Rita S., and Deborah S. Romaine. *The Complete Idiot's Guide to Communicating with Spirits*. Royersford, PA: Alpha, 2002.

Bryan, Jessica. *Psychic Surgery and Faith Healing: An Exploration of Multi-Dimensional Realities, Indigenous Healing, and Medical Miracles in the Philippine Lowlands*. San Francisco: Red Wheel/Weiser/Conari, 2008.

   * Jessica Bryan is featured in chapter 11

Edward, John. *Crossing Over: The Stories Behind the Stories*. San Diego, CA: Jodere Group, 2001.

Guggenheim, Bill, and Judy Guggenheim, *Hello from Heaven: A New Field of Research-After-Death Communication Confirms That Life and Love Are Eternal*. New York: Bantam, 1997.

Holland, John. *Born Knowing*. Carlsbad, CA: Hay House, 2003.

Stefanidakis, Rev. Simeon. *How to Develop Mediumship and Channeling*, 5th ed. Boston: Self published, 2001.

Van Praagh, James. *Talking to Heaven*. New York: Dutton, 1997.

Resources on the Web

Bob Olsen's Site for Healing Mind, Body, Spirit *www.ofspirit.com*

Chanda Parkinson *www.chandaparkinson.com*

Explore Astrology with Sheri Woxland *www.astrowork.com*

The First Spiritual Temple *www.fst.org*

Forever Family Foundation *www.foreverfamilyfoundation.org*

Grief Pioneer Elisabeth Kubler Ross *www.elisabethkublerross.com*

The Spiritual Cinema Circle *www.spiritualcinemacircle.com*

*For more information, stories, and behind the scenes
photos and videos*

Check out
www.troyparkinson.com